The
Perfect Basket

The
Perfect Basket

How to Make a Fabulous Gift Basket for Any Occasion

DIANE PHILLIPS

THE HARVARD COMMON PRESS

BOSTON, MASSACHUSETTS

The Harvard Common Press
535 Albany Street
Boston, Massachusetts 02118
www.harvardcommonpress.com

Printed in China

Printed on acid-free paper

Library of Congress Cataloging-in-Publication Data

Phillips, Diane.
  The perfect basket : how to make a fabulous gift basket for any occasion / Diane Phillips.
    p. cm.
  ISBN 1-55832-294-9 (pbk. : alk. paper)
  1. Handicraft. 2. Cookery. 3. Gift baskets. I. Title.
  TT157.P4653 2005
  745.59—dc22   2005004439

ISBN-13: 978-1-55832-294-3
ISBN-10: 1-55832-294-9

Special bulk-order discounts are available on this and other Harvard Common Press books. Companies and organizations may purchase books for premiums or resale, or may arrange a custom edition, by contacting the Marketing Director at the address above.

10 9 8 7 6 5 4 3 2 1

Book design by Night & Day Design
Photo styling by Christine McCabe

DEDICATION

To my agent, Susan Ginsburg, who is not only
a great friend, but is also the best cookbook
agent on the planet—I am grateful for all that
she does for me each day.

ACKNOWLEDGMENTS

Gift giving is a part of the fabric of my life. Whether it's giving a gift basket, a loaf of bread, or my time to a cause, giving to others gives me great joy. That being said, this book would not have been possible without the generosity others have bestowed upon me.

To my husband, Chuck, who will graciously take me out to dinner after a long day of testing and writing, a special thank you for your understanding and love. To our children, Ryan and Carrie, thanks for sharing your lives with us and for being such terrific adults—I am overwhelmed by your successes.

Thanks to the friends who have encouraged me along the way: Christine Willems, Jan Stapp, Suzie Rantzow, Muffie Knox, Loraine Lukash, Roberta Hestenes, Nonnie and Bruce Owens, and our Sunday night group, who were always up for a new taste or adventure.

Thanks also to my cousins Bob and Donna Pasquin and their gracious family, whose friendship and hospitality have been such a gift.

Teaching in cities across the country, I have met many friends who have become part of my family when I am on the road. Special thanks to: Chan Patterson and the staffs at the Viking Culinary Arts Centers and Viking Home Chef; Bob Nemorovski and the family at Ramekins; Cynthia Liu, Mia Chambers, and the staffs at Draegers; Doralece Dullaghan and the Staffs at Sur La Table; Marilyn Markel and the staff at A Southern Season; Larry Oats and the staff at KitchenArt; Nancy Pigg, Lana Santavicca, Nancy Rau, and the Fricke family at CooksWares; Sue and Lynn Hoffman and the angels at the Kitchen Shoppe; and the staffs at Central Markets. A special thank you to Ron and Devora Eisenberg, Allison Sherwood, Erika D'Eugenio, Sara Rose, and the amazing staff and volunteers at Great News! in San Diego for giving me a kitchen to call home.

At The Harvard Common Press, thanks to my publisher, Bruce Shaw, and to the rest of the staff there: Christine Alaimo, Liza Beth, Valerie Cimino, Abby Collier, Christine Corcoran Cox, Virginia Downes, Amy Etcheson, Pat Jalbert-Levine, Skye Stewart, Julie Strane, Megan Weireter, and Betsy Young. I am grateful for all your hard work to make this book so beautiful and for taking it into the marketplace. I am privileged to work with such a wonderful group of professionals, who also enjoy a good laugh! Thanks also to Barb Jatkola for her great job copyediting; this book is better for your keen eye and great questions.

CONTENTS

INTRODUCTION

I love giving gifts. Whether it's a beautiful crystal vase filled with flowers from my garden or a basket filled with home-baked goodies, it's a labor of love when I think about the recipient and how I'd like to show him or her my appreciation and affection. I began giving gift baskets to my friends and family when my children were young and I didn't have a lot of disposable income. The children are grown now, but the idea of giving a basket filled with things that I think my friends will enjoy is still a part of my life.

I wrote the original edition of *The Perfect Basket* in 1994, when the gift basket industry was just beginning. It was a book that gave readers inspiration and ideas for creating their own gift baskets filled with homemade treats or purchased items built around a theme. Today gift baskets are a $2.8 billion industry—a pretty staggering figure if you know how much each item in a basket is typically worth. But this is not a book about how to start your own gift basket business—there are lots of sources for learning about that. *The Perfect Basket* is written to inspire you to make your own baskets for family and friends. Putting together themed baskets to give to loved ones as a personal expression of your affection and gratitude will give you a feeling of joy and satisfaction that handing them a gift card to the local department store could never replicate.

What's different about this book is the range of choices I give for putting together a basket. Whether you want to give something as simple as a mug filled with a homemade coffee or chocolate drink or an over the top basket with mugs, an espresso machine, assorted coffees, chocolate spoons, and flavored syrups, you'll be able to use each basket idea to create an inexpensive or a splurge gift, or anything in between, by adding or subtracting a few items.

Containers for your gift baskets don't have to be limited to the usual wicker baskets; rather, they can be any number of items that will fit the theme.

For example, a plastic bucket can hold all the items for a new car basket, such as car washing soap, a chamois, and the like. A soup tureen will hold soup mixes, a bundt pan will hold cake mixes, a salad spinner can hold flavored vinegars and herb blends for salad, breadbaskets or loaf pans can hold bread mixes, and a cookie jar can hold cookie mixes. You should use this book for inspiration and then put your own stamp on the gifts themselves, changing the containers to suit your preferences and your pocketbook.

There are two sections in *The Perfect Basket*. The first is about giving themed special occasion baskets filled with store-bought items that you will arrange in a container and present to your recipient. These baskets celebrate an occasion, such as a new car, a honeymoon, a new pet, or a special trip. These special occasion baskets range in price from around $25 to upward of $100, with various price points in between, so you can mix and match the items on the list to fit your budget and personal preferences. To make sure you have flexibility when tailoring these gifts to your friends and family, I provide lots of choices for items to fill each basket, as well as different prices for different versions of the same basket.

The second section of *The Perfect Basket* is made up of food-related gifts. Because I'm a cookbook author and teacher, these gifts are near and dear to my heart, and they are some of my favorite ways to remember friends and family. Each of these baskets has a mix of some kind, and a recipe for preparing the mix, to include with other items. This chapter is also full of choices. You can follow exactly the basket suggestions I have provided, or you can mix and match mixes and recipes to create your own baskets. You can also tailor any given basket according to the kind of present you want to give: a simple soup mix

Tip: No matter what you are using for your container, make sure to place heavier items in the bottom and arrange smaller, lighter, and more fragile items on top.

tucked into a large mug makes a great gift for your child's teacher, or you can give an entire soup and bread basket, packed into a gleaming new stockpot, to a favorite relative.

For both of these sections, the type of container you choose will affect the overall price of the gift. The most economical choice is a plain brown or white grocery bag or a plain box that you have on hand, which you can decorate with stickers, markers, paints, wrapping paper, and the like. An attractive heavy-duty gift bag from a card store or an inexpensive canvas tote bag from a craft store might cost between $3 and $10. Straw and wood baskets are available in that price range from craft stores. Using a piece of cookware, a backpack, or a picnic hamper for the container may cost significantly more. For the basic baskets, I have estimated between $5 and $10 for the cost of the container and have noted where other options will increase the total price of the gift. Again, I've tried to give you many choices in each situation.

General Guidelines for Filling Baskets

The size and depth of your container will give you an idea of how it should be filled. One rule of thumb is that it's better to buy a small container and really stuff it than to have just a few items swimming around in a large container. Having said that, there are many ways to fill out that large basket so it doesn't look so bare. Here are some of my favorite tips for filling baskets.

1. Varied containers are widely available either from housewares stores or gift basket supply houses, which you can find in the Source Guide on page 137. My favorite places to scour are discount department stores such as HomeGoods and import stores such as Pier 1 Imports and Cost Plus World Market, but don't limit yourself. There are many other treasure-troves, such as Ikea, flea markets, craft stores such as Michaels, and the Container Store, where I can get lost just looking for possibilities. And don't forget factory outlet stores.

2. Tissue, cellophane, and boxes, as well as decorative tins, are all available on the Internet from gift basket supply companies or through well-known retailers such as the Baker's Catalogue from King Arthur Flour, the Container Store, Ikea, Hallmark stores, Williams-Sonoma, and Sur La Table. Your local cake decorating store will also carry many of these items.

3. Make sure to fill the container with excelsior (curved wood shavings used for packing) or straw to give height to the contents so that the recipient can see what's actually in there. This is especially important for bowls, stockpots, buckets, and other deep containers.

4. If you are using a heavy paper gift bag for your container, stuff the bag with lots of colored tissue paper to raise the level of the contents.

5. No matter what you are using for your container, make sure to place heavier items in the bottom and arrange smaller, lighter, and more fragile items on top.

6. Check the gift mix recipes ahead of time to be sure you buy the correct size containers. I give the measurements for the mixes in cups. If fitting something in a certain container might be close, buy the next size up.

7. When packing a food-related gift basket, remember what's referred to as "shelf stability." That is the length of time the item can be stored at room temperature before it will no longer be usable. This is particularly true with a baking mix, which you will want to label with an expiration date, as well as foods such as vacuum-packed salami and crackers. Make sure to tell the recipient if the items are fresh and need to be refrigerated or how they should be stored. In general, a spice blend can last on the shelf for four to six months, baking mixes with leavening in them about three months.

8. Position your items in the basket in a tentative arrangement. You may have to move things around until you feel that everything is in the right spot. Then wrap the entire basket in cellophane, tie it up with streamer ribbons, and tuck something that coordinates with the theme through the ribbons. This could be crossed wooden spoons for a cooking basket or shells tied to the ribbons for a beach-themed basket. You could also attach the ends of two kitchen towels to the bottom of the container with double-sided tape, then bring the ends up to the top of the container and tie them together. These special touches will make the basket appear full. Just look at some of those prepared

Tip: Make sure to fill the container with excelsior or straw to give height to the contents so that the recipient can see what's actually in there. This is especially important for bowls, stockpots, buckets, and other deep containers.

baskets in your local gift store—there may not be that much in them, but they look beautiful!

9. Don't forget a card. This final touch completes the basket. You can use colored card stock (available at most office supply stores) and make your own card on the computer or by hand, tying it in with the theme and/or color of the basket. You can also use a pretty store-bought card.

Ready and Waiting

I'm always of the mind that to do anything well, you should have a few really good tools ready and waiting for those spur-of-the-moment occasions. Here are some items I always keep in my gift-giving closet.

- Wired ribbon in different colors
- Streamer ribbons that can be curled with scissors
- Grosgrain ribbon in different widths and colors
- Bows, or ribbons to make bows
- Ceramic paints for mugs and plates
- Fabric paints
- Sharpie markers
- Colored markers
- Seasonal stickers
- Rubber stamps and stamp pads
- Silk flowers or vines
- Pinecones
- Sprigs of dried herbs
- Tissue paper
- Cellophane bags
- Cellophane wrap in various colors
- Recycled jars
- Boxes (save any that would make nice containers)
- Wrapping paper

Tip: Check the gift mix recipes ahead of time to be sure you buy the correct size containers. I give the measurements for the mixes in cups. If fitting something in a certain container might be close, buy the next size up.

- Card stock for copying recipes or making cards
- Hole punch
- Glue gun
- White glue or craft glue
- Fabric scraps (for decorating boxes or fitting over jar tops)
- Scissors (for fabric and for paper)
- Pinking shears

Enjoy!

My last tip is, have fun! Giving gifts should fill you with joy. Think about the person (or persons) you are making this gift for and enjoy the process of personalizing it and producing something he or she will truly enjoy. This can also be a teaching moment for your children. If your child has a favorite teacher, coach, babysitter, or dance instructor, the child can be part of the gift-giving process, choosing just the right container and its contents. Whether you have a few dollars to spend or can afford a lot more, baskets are gifts to give from your heart and home, and they reflect that you have given some thought, time, and effort to show the recipients how much you appreciate them.

SPECIAL OCCASION BASKETS

Spa Basket

Say Cheese Basket

Junk Drawer Remedy Basket

Warm Welcome to the
Neighborhood Basket

Bread Baking Basket

Cookie Baking Basket

Washday Basket

Baby's Here Basket

Toddler Basket

Stroller Basket

Sous Chef Basket

Beer Lover's Basket

Tailgating Basket

Camper's Backpack

On the Road Again Basket

New Car Basket

Sewing Basket

Off to College Basket

Teen Summer Survival Kit

Sun and Sand Basket

Book Lover's Basket

Asian Flavors Basket

Cake Baking Basket

Teddy Bear Picnic Basket

Grill Master Basket

Sunday Painter Basket

Thanks for the Memories Basket

Music Lover's Basket

Honeymooners' Basket

Wine and Cheese Basket

Guest's Bedside Basket

Hearth and Home Basket

A Bit of Britain Basket

Get Well Basket

Hostess with the Mostest Basket

Assistant's Basket

Boss's Retreat Basket

New Pet Basket

Back to School Basket

Apple for the Teacher Basket

Got the Munchies Basket

Beach House Basket

Saturday Night at the Movies
Basket

Après-Ski Basket

Boater's Basket

Guy Golfer's Basket

Lady Golfer's Basket

Petite Picasso Basket

Sports Fan Basket

Tennis Basket

Fun and Games Basket

Gardener's Helper Basket

Bird Watcher's Basket

Writing Desk Basket

Fiesta Basket

Well-Stocked Pot Basket

Martini Basket

Well-Stocked Bar Basket

Slow Cooker Basket

Clambake Basket

Picnic Basket

Little Red Wagon

Guest's Bath Basket

Taste of the Tropics Basket

Festival Italiano Basket

Tool Time Basket

This section is for all of us who enjoy giving gifts to commemorate special events in family and friends' lives, whether big or small. These occasions can include birthdays and the like, when you may give gifts highlighting hobbies, but they can also include moving into a new apartment, buying a car, going on a tailgating expedition, or adopting a new pet.

For each basket in this section, I have estimated a baseline container cost of between $5 and $10. The cost estimates for the completed baskets include the container itself, along with the suggested items to include. That said, you may find more expensive or less expensive containers, and your final basket may in fact cost more or less than my basic price. Some items, such as the rolling cooler for the tailgate basket, will clearly hike up the price dramatically, so I have also suggested other, less expensive items to use instead. And in some cases I have suggested more items under a particular price point than you may end up including, because I want to give you some options.

I love to scour discount stores such as Marshalls and Ross Stores to find items to include in baskets, and these stores, along with the others mentioned in the Source Guide (page 137), can be great resources for baskets, tote bags, and other items that can serve as containers and decorations. There are all kinds of places to shop and lots of ways to economize, which is why I give you a range of costs for the items in each basket. Some may cost more than what I've estimated, and some may cost less, depending on the stores in your area. As I said before, be creative and shop for sales. If a fabric decorated with hearts is on sale in October, buy it with the idea that you'll use it in February to line a sweetheart basket or wrap packages of cookie mix and heart-shaped cookie cutters. I'm always picking up items when they are on sale so that I can use them at a later date, and it's a good habit to get into.

Conventional baskets aren't the only containers that you can use when designing a gift basket. Canvas or plastic Jelly-type tote bags, wooden boxes, laundry baskets, hampers, backpacks, magazine racks, log baskets, lap trays, small vegetable baskets, flowerpots, buckets, toolboxes, and myriad other items can be adapted to your gift-giving needs.

Decorating your package is a nice way to personalize it. Stickers, rubber stamp designs, and confetti can all be used to design a personal gift. Use stencils and fabric or ceramic paints to personalize mugs and fabrics. You can cover an ordinary box with fabric using a glue gun; cover the box with several layers of tissue paper and paint it with a water-soluble polyurethane to get an easy decoupage look; or decoupage old postcards to the outside of the box. Fabric-lined boxes and baskets are simple to construct, using a glue gun to attach the fabric to a box or basket. If the basket has handles, weave ribbons through the handles for an upscale look. Put your personal stamp on the gift. Whether you are crafty and want to go all out or you can't glue-gun your way out of a craft shop, you can put together delightful baskets for all your family and friends by following my suggestions and making these baskets your own.

Spa Basket

Everyone needs a little TLC, and this pampering basket is just what the doctor ordered for a stressed-out friend or for Mom on Mother's Day. Line a basket with a bath towel of an appropriate color, then wrap each item individually in tissue paper and tie the packages with grosgrain ribbon. Weave coordinating ribbon through the handles of the basket. You can also cover a box with fabric or wrapping paper and then stuff the box or basket with excelsior, which you can find in any gift, card, or craft store.

Basic Basket
(under $25)

Loofah

Nail brush

Bath beads

Bubble bath

Body lotion

Magazines

More Than Basic Basket
(under $50)—add the following

Back scrubber

Manicure set

Scented candle with holder

The Works
(around $100)— add the following

Washcloths and hand towels

CDs of soothing music

Terry cloth robe

Say Cheese Basket

This delicious basket needs to be given within a day of being packed. Make sure to let the recipient know that he or she should refrigerate the cheese wedges immediately. Otherwise, I would send this basket without the cheeses and include a gift certificate to a local cheese shop. Start with a nice basket, line it with a pretty napkin, and then fill it with straw and your items. The basket can be reused to serve crackers.

Basic Basket
(around $30)

Wedges of 2 different cheeses

Boxes of assorted crackers to complement the cheeses

Cloth or paper cocktail napkins

Set of cheese knives (a cheese plane, slicer, and spreader)

Cheese tags for printing the names of the cheeses

More Than Basic Basket
(around $60)— add the following

Another wedge of cheese

Cheese board (marble, wood, or bamboo)

Jar of cornichons (little sour French pickles)

Jar of pickled onions

Jar of assorted olives

The Works
(around $100)— add the following

Book about serving cheese

Gift certificate to local cheese shop

2 bottles of wine to complement the cheeses

2 wineglasses

Junk Drawer Remedy Basket

Everyone has that drawer in the kitchen or workshop that collects everything from extra pens and pencils to odds and ends. This basket is what I call the kitchen table office, and it will give your friend a place to store all those things necessary to run the house without clogging up a drawer or countertop. Use small, square plastic berry baskets to hold some of the smaller items, and nest these into a tray or shallow box. You can also get great ideas for containers at an office supply store, where you will find all the items necessary for the basket. This is a terrific housewarming or wedding shower gift.

Basic Basket
(under $25)

Package of pencils

Assorted pens (in colors), markers, or highlighters

Plain paper

Envelopes

Roll of postage stamps

Sticky notes

Scotch tape

Small stapler

Coupon file for grocery coupons

Small calculator

Scissors

More Than Basic Basket
(over $50)—add the following

Address book

Ruler

Rubber stamps and stamp pads (in colors)

Small calligraphy pen set

Initial seal with wax

Note cards for thank-you notes and other correspondence

Warm Welcome to the Neighborhood Basket

Your new neighbors have just moved in. They are surrounded by boxes and appear dazed and lost. You show up with this terrific basket filled with things they will need to get acquainted with the neighborhood. Consider yourself the Welcome Wagon! A nice basket is terrific for this gift; your neighbors will be able to reuse it to collect mail or arrange fruit. For city information, log on to your local community's Web site to download information about refuse collection and where to call for newspaper delivery, cable, and other services.

Basic Basket
(around $25)

Map(s) of the area

Subscription to local newspaper or magazine

Card listing store recommendations, local services, and when trash is collected (they will need to get rid of those boxes!)

Card listing your favorite restaurants (and phone numbers if they deliver), dry cleaners, baby-sitters, and your phone number or other information

Granola or snack bars, bottles of water, and apples or other fresh fruit

More Than Basic Basket
(around $50)— add the following

Movie theater gift certificates

Grocery store gift certificate

Bread Baking Basket

This basket is for the more veteran baker. Start with a pretty mixing bowl and place tissue paper in the bottom, then fill with the bread baking essentials.

Basic Basket
(around $25)

Spatula

SAF yeast

Instant-read thermometer

More Than Basic Basket
(around $50)— add the following

Angled measuring cup

Measuring spoons

Bread pans

The Works
(around $100)— add the following

Basic baking book

5-pound bag of King Arthur Flour

Breadboard

Serrated bread knife

Over the Top Basket *(around $200)—add the following*

Bread machine

Cookie Baking Basket

There is nothing better than a homemade cookie (although at my house, frozen Oreos will do in a pinch). This basket is for your favorite baker; you can update his or her baking equipment with just a few items. I like to assemble this gift in a jellyroll pan and then wrap the entire thing in cellophane and tie it with streamer ribbons, securing the center of the ribbons with two crossed spatulas.

Basic Basket
(around $25)

Silicone baking mat for jellyroll pan

Scoops of varying sizes for cookies

Chocolate chips

More Than Basic Basket
(around $60)— add the following

Heatproof spatula

Microplane grater

Basic cookie cookbook

Assorted extracts or baking oils (vanilla, lemon, orange)

Chopped nuts

Potholders

Washday Basket

This is just the gift for the person who is moving into his or her first apartment. Fill a large, colorful laundry bag or basket with these essentials.

Basic Basket
(around $30)

Laundry detergent

All-fabric bleach

Fabric softener

Stain stick or remover

Roll of quarters

More Than Basic Basket
(around $50)— add the following

Liquid soap for delicate fabrics

Mesh bag for delicate clothes

24 plastic hangers

Drying rack

The Works
(around $75)— add the following

Steam iron

Tabletop ironing board

Baby's Here Basket

Welcome a newborn with this assortment of baby basics, given in a portable baby bathtub. Line the tub with a hooded bath towel and arrange the items in the tub, tying thin satin ribbon around each one, or wrap each in tissue paper. Soft items look cute rolled and tied with ribbon. Another great container idea is a diaper bag.

Basic Basket
(around $30)

Baby washcloth

Hooded bath towel

Baby soap

Baby shampoo

Baby nail clippers

Diaper rash ointment

More Than Basic Basket
(around $50)— add the following

Baby lotion

Disposable cameras

Package of newborn disposable diapers

Baby sleeper

Brush and comb

Rattle

The Works
(around $100)— add the following

Rubber duck

Stuffed animal

Snugli baby carrier

Disposable bottles

Pacifier

Teether

Over the Top Basket *($150 and up)—add the following*

Baby Einstein videos or DVDs and audio CDs

Toddler Basket

This gift is for an older child who is able to sit up and eat in a highchair. Pack the items in a small stackable tote that can be kept near a highchair or used later for toy storage. After placing the individually wrapped items in the tote, wrap the whole thing in a small plastic tablecloth that can be slipped under and around the highchair at mealtime to protect the floor and catch food spills. The cloth is then easily wiped down for another use. This is a great basket to give to grandparents for when grand-children come to visit.

Basic Basket
(around $25)

2 bibs

2 baby spoons

Baby bowl

Compartmentalized baby plate

Lidded cup

Small squeeze toy with suction base for highchair tray

Small plastic book for "reading" at mealtime

Baby wipes

Stroller Basket

For this gift, I like to use a tote bag that is zippered, so that when it's used, the contents won't fall out. But you can certainly use an open canvas tote, if you'd like. This tote is packed full of all the things new parents need when they venture off into the world with their precious cargo. Whether they use it for a car trip to the store or a walk through the park, they will love you for your thoughtfulness.

Basic Basket
(around $25)

Disposable diapers

Changing pad

Baby wipes

Zipper-top plastic bags

Travel bottle

More Than Basic Basket
(around $50)— add the following

Bib

Burp cloth or cloth diaper

Pacifier

Teething toy

Rattle

Lightweight blanket

The Works
(around $100)— add the following

Sun hat or knit hat for cooler weather

Baby sunglasses

Baby sunblock

Small bottled water

Small box of tissues

Stain remover wipes

Small board books

Disposable cameras

Sous Chef Basket

Help a novice cook equip a kitchen by providing some basic tools. Since the tools have handles, make a bouquet by tying them together with ribbon and placing them upright in a crock, or put them in the basket of a dish drainer. Larger items can be arranged in a dish drainer or given in a basket. If you are giving both the crock and the larger items, place the crock in a large basket, then add the other items to the basket.

Basic Basket
(around $25 with crock)

Wire sauce whisk

2 heatproof spatulas

3 wooden or fiberglass stirring spoons

Ladle

Slotted spoon

Long meat fork

Tongs (2 sizes)

More Than Basic Basket
(around $50)— add one or more of the following

Paring knife

Vegetable peeler

Manual can opener

Kitchen scissors

Serrated knife

The Works
(around $100)— add one or more of the following

Small plastic cutting board

Nested set of mixing bowls

Hand-held cheese grater or microplane grater

Measuring cups and spoons

Corkscrew

Basic cookbook

Beer Lover's Basket

I won't suggest this for the college student in your life, but there are friends who would love this addition to their apartments or homes. Start with a galvanized tub of an appropriate size and fill it with straw, then include your favorite items from the list. Wrap the whole thing in cellophane and tie a bottle opener to the streamer ribbons.

Basic Basket
(around $25)

Beer mugs or steins

Nuts and other salty snacks

Bottle opener

More Than Basic Basket
(around $60)— add one or more of the following

Assorted beers

Pilsner glasses

Membership in or gift certificate to World Beer Direct (see Source Guide)

Tailgating Basket

This gift is for a friend who has season tickets for the local football or baseball team. This person is serious about sports and would love a rolling cooler filled with all these items. Since the cooler is a pricey container, you could also use a plastic box or basket for this gift.

Basic Basket
(around $25 if not using the rolling cooler)

Bag of pretzels

Bag of peanuts

Bag of popcorn

Six-packs of soda and beer

Team hat

More Than Basic Basket
(around $50)— add the following

40-quart rolling cooler

The Works
(around $100)— add one or more of the following

Team jersey

Plastic cups with team logo

Tear-apart referee doll

Season's program for favorite team

Gift certificate to team store

Camper's Backpack

Designed for the novice or experienced camper, this out-fitted backpack is filled with just the right basics to take along on a trip to the great outdoors.

Basic Basket
(around $30)

Flashlight

Water bottle

Folded plastic poncho

Compass

More Than Basic Basket
(around $50)— add the following

Swiss Army knife or Leatherman tool

The Works
(around $75)— add the following

Batteries

Trail mix

Hiking guide for local area

Over the Top Basket *(around $500)—add the following*

Hand-held Global Positioning System (GPS) device

Gift certificate to local camping store

Battery-operated lantern

Disposable cameras

On the Road Again Basket

When I was a child, my parents took the family on many long driving trips. My aunt used to pack baskets with things for us to do in the car. The rule for our trips was that we could unwrap only one item at a time, and at given intervals we were allowed to open others. Keeping track on the car clock helped us learn to tell time. When selecting items, consider the gender and age of the children as well as the length of the trip. To hold the items, my first choice is a backpack, with each item inside wrapped in colored tissue paper. Less expensive options would be a Jelly-type plastic tote for a girl, a G.I. Joe camouflage bag for a boy, or even a sturdy gift bag from a card store.

Basic Basket
(around $25)

Drawing/writing pad

Washable crayons or markers

Coloring book

Playing cards

Rubber stamps and stamp pads

Travel-size games

More Than Basic Basket
(around $50)— add one or more of the following

Small portable cassette or CD player with extra batteries

Prerecorded cassettes or CDs

The Works
(around $100)— add the following

Books (including book of car games and activities)

Disposable cameras

Map to keep track of the trip

Travel diary and pencil

Stamps for postcards

New Car Basket

My husband is a car fanatic. His cars are immaculate, and Lord help the person who rubs up against them. For Christmas one year, one of his favorite gifts was a plastic bucket filled with car cleaning equipment. Give this to a friend who has just bought a new car or a teenager who has just gotten his or her driver's license.

Basic Basket
(around $25 with bucket)

Chamois

Car washing sponge and soap

Car wax

Interior upholstery cleaner

Tire cleaner

Tire brush

Window and vinyl cleaner

More Than Basic Basket
(around $50)— add the following

Key chain

Flashlight

Spare key compartment

Road maps

The Works
(over $100)—add one or more of the following

Gift certificate to local car wash

Gift certificate to local gas station

Automobile club membership

Jumper cables

First-aid kit

Driving gloves

Sewing Basket

Sewing seems to be a dying art, but we all need to sew on a button, mend a sweater, or fix a tear in a pair of jeans now and then. This cute little gift is best when it's given in a basket or small box with a lid. Try to find one that has pretty fabric on the outside and inside, then fill it with mending essentials. This makes a great gift for a student going off to college, a new neighbor, or an old friend.

Basic Basket
(around $30)

Assorted thread in basic colors (white, ecru, navy, black, and brown)

Assorted needles

Pincushion

Stainless steel straight pins

Safety pins

Small package of assorted shirt buttons

Packages of hooks and eyes and snaps

Strip of Velcro

Good pair of fabric scissors

More Than Basic Basket
(around $50)— add the following

Pinking shears

Fabric chalk

Basic sewing book

Measuring tape

Off to College Basket

This basket is an ideal gift to give to a recent high-school grad on his or her way to college. Since there isn't much space in a dorm room, pack everything into a plastic crate that can be reused for storage.

Basic Basket
(around $35)

Journal and pens

Roll of quarters for laundry

Stationery, post-cards, and stamps

Pocket-size day planner

More Than Basic Basket
(around $50)— add one or more of the following

Wall calendar highlighted with special family dates and events

Granola or energy bars

Clock radio

The Works
($75 and up)— add one or more of the following

Portable CD player or iPod

Gift certificate to Amazon.com

Stuffed animal

Wall posters

Prepaid calling card

Disposable cameras

Teen Summer Survival Kit

School is out and it's time to enjoy the beach, so what better gift for a birthday or graduation than one that is filled with summer essentials? Pack these into a beach bag and coordinate all the items around the colors of the bag.

Basic Basket
(around $25)

Beach towel

Sunblock

Flip-flops

Frisbee

More Than Basic Basket
(around $50)— add one or more of the following

Gift certificate to local music store or Amazon.com

Books or gift certificate to local bookstore

The Works
($75 to $100)— add the following

Sunglasses

Plain visor and puffy paints to decorate it with

Gift certificate to local movie theater

Beach mat

T-shirt or sweatshirt

Disposable cameras

Sun and Sand Basket

My family lives near the beach, so our beach basket is always filled and ready to go. A natural as a housewarming gift for the new owners of a beach home, this basket also makes a sunny sendoff for seaside honeymooners. For a couple, divide the items into two packages and give his-and-hers matching totes. I love the large canvas totes from L.L.Bean and Lands' End for this gift basket, and they can be monogrammed. A sturdy gift bag from a card store will help keep costs down.

Basic Basket
(around $40)

2 beach towels

2 roll-up beach mats

Sunblock

More Than Basic Basket
(around $60)— add one or more of the following

Sunglasses

Hats or visors

Inflatable beach ball

Frisbee

Travel-size Scrabble game

The Works
($100 to $150)— add the following

Underwater masks and snorkels

CD player

Water bottles

Beach chairs

Disposable cameras

Book Lover's Basket

Some people just love books, collecting as well as reading them. This basket is for someone who appreciates the written word and enjoys reading. It makes a great birthday present for a special friend or going-away gift for a neighbor or coworker. I like to present this in a simple box covered with wrapping paper that looks like library shelves. Arrange all the items in the box and cover with cellophane. Tie with streamer ribbons and attach bookmarks to the center bow.

Basic Basket
(around $25)
Bookmarks
Bookplates
Nice pen to label bookplates
Journal
Book that you know the person would love to read

More Than Basic Basket
(around $50)—add one or more of the following
Gift certificate to local bookstore
Bookends
Small book light
Magnifying glass (if the person has trouble reading fine print)
Embosser to label books

The Works
(around $100)—add one or more of the following
Lap desk or back pillow for reading in bed
Tickets to local writers' conference or poetry reading
Autographed copy of favorite author's work
Gift certificate to Levenger catalog or store (see Source Guide)

Asian Flavors Basket

This basket is actually a bamboo steamer filled with Asian ingredients and utensils to spur the recipient's creativity in the kitchen. You can certainly substitute a wok for the steamer or add a wok to the mix; it's up to you and your pocketbook. Wrap the basket in cellophane and then decorate it with streamer ribbons, inserting crossed chopsticks through the center of the ribbons.

Basic Basket
(around $30 with steamer or wok)
Stir-fry paddle
Bag of sticky rice
Soy sauce
Toasted sesame oil
Rice wine (mirin)
Rice paddle

4 sets of chopsticks
4 chopstick rests

More Than Basic Basket
(around $50)—add the following
4 rice bowls
4 sauce dishes
Set of cooking chopsticks

Basic Asian cookbook

The Works
(around $100)—add the following
Rice cooker and/or wok or steamer (depending on what you've already included)

Cake Baking Basket

This basket begins with a sturdy mixing bowl and is filled with all the essentials for great cake baking. It makes a nice wedding shower or birthday gift.

Basic Basket
(around $30)

Offset spatulas (2 sizes)

Small set of tips for frosting

2 disposable pastry bags

Cupcake liners

Cake flour

More Than Basic Basket
(around $60)— add the following

Two 9-inch cake pans or one 13 x 9-inch baking dish

Heatproof spatula

Sprinkles for decorating

Basic cake cookbook

The Works
(around $100)— add the following

Hand mixer

Microplane grater

Balloon whisk

Potholders

Muffin tins

Over the Top Basket *($300 to $400)—add the following*

Instead of hand mixer, KitchenAid stand mixer

Teddy Bear Picnic Basket

A charming idea for a child's birthday party, this basket, with its cuddly teddy bear theme, will delight boys and girls alike. Make sure to decorate the party area with teddy bears of all shapes and descriptions. For a basic container, use white paper lunch sacks with bear-related rubber stamps or stickers. For the works, line a large picnic basket with bear-motif fabric or wrapping paper.

Basic Basket
(around $10 per child)

Bear ears for each guest (available at party shops)

Box of teddy bear cookies for each guest

Bag of gummy bears for each guest

Paper plates, cups, and napkins with bear theme

More Than Basic Basket
(around $25 per child)—add the following

Small teddy bear for each guest

Grill Master Basket

This is a nice gift to give someone who loves the thrill of the grill. Start with a vegetable grilling basket, then load that with all the goodies necessary for a great grilling experience. Wrap it up in cellophane or a humorous apron for the grill master.

Basic Basket
(around $25)

Assorted wood chips for smoking

Assorted rubs or marinades for grilling

Extra-virgin olive oil

Long heatproof hand mitts

Grill brush for cleaning the grill

More Than Basic Basket
(around $60)—add one or more of the following

Kebab skewers (these can range from bamboo to fancy metal)

Set of grilling tools

Silicone basting brush

Basic grilling book

The Works
(around $100)—add one or more of the following

Personalized branding iron

Clip-on grill lamp

Small fire extinguisher

Sunday Painter Basket

This starter kit for watercolor painting is perfect to give to a workaholic or someone beginning retirement. It fits nicely in a fishing tackle box with a hinged lid, a handle, and an interior compartment for separating brushes and tubes of paint.

Basic Basket
(around $30)

Basic assortment of tube watercolors

Paintbrushes in assorted sizes

Watercolor pencils

Erasers

Sketchbook

Block of watercolor paper

More Than Basic Basket
(around $50)—add the following

Pastel crayons

Apron or painting smock

Paint rags

How-to book on watercolor painting

Water bottles for cleaning brushes

The Works
($50 and up)—add the following

Gift certificate to art classes at local school

Gift certificate to local art store

Polaroid camera with film

Thanks for the Memories Basket

This basket is actually a box for helping a friend organize his or her photographs or start taking photographs. We all know someone who could use this basket. I like to use a large box—either a hatbox that has a decorative exterior or another box with a lid that you can decorate yourself.

Basic Basket
(around $30)

Large photo album that can accommodate additional inserts

Photograph labels

Sharpie markers for labeling photos

Boxes to store photos, with date separators

More Than Basic Basket
(around $50)— add one or more of the following

Disposable cameras

Small frames for special photos

Paper to record special memories (most stationery stores have nice paper that can even be used with a computer printer)

Additional inserts for the photo album

The Works
(around $100)— add the following

Gift certificate to local photo finishing store for restoration of old photos

Book on storing and arranging photos

Music Lover's Basket

This basket can be put together for a youngster, teenager, or adult—just tailor your selections and container to the person's musical tastes. It makes a great birthday present or a wedding shower gift for a couple. I like to load all these goodies into a nylon tote bag or backpack, but a nice covered box that can be used to store CDs works well, too.

Basic Basket
(around $40)

Selection of CDs

Gift certificate to local music store

Notebook-style CD holder

More Than Basic Basket
(around $75)— add one or more of the following

Music posters

Book about type of music recipient most enjoys

Portable CD player

Gift certificate for music downloads from iTunes Music Store or other online retailer

Honeymooners' Basket

This basket reminds me of those you might see in an old movie as a cruise ship departs and everyone is drinking champagne and nibbling on caviar. You can re-create this getaway basket for newlyweds (or friends who are going on a trip) by lining a large basket or tray with straw or Mylar and filling it with extravagant delicacies.

Basic Basket
(around $50)

Bottle of champagne

2 champagne flutes

Jar of caviar

Package of assorted crackers

More Than Basic Basket
(around $75)—add the following

Assorted fresh or dried fruit

Jar of truffle paste

Assorted chocolates

Tour book of destination

Disposable cameras

Wine and Cheese Basket

This unique basket is a great wedding shower or anniversary gift. Pack the items in a round basket filled with Mylar, wrap it in clear cellophane, and decorate it with streamer ribbons. The baskets listed do not include any wine (or cheese), but a great idea is to get a group of friends together to buy a wine rack and wines to go in it and give the rack along with the basket. This would be an investment gift, a little over the top in terms of price, but the bride and groom will have vintages to open on special anniversaries. Select a wooden or steel wine rack and have your local wine shop help you choose some wines that will mature in time for your friends' first, fifth, tenth, and ongoing milestone anniversaries. Label the bottles for those occasions and fill the rest of the rack with other fine mature wines.

Basic Basket
(around $30)

Subscription to food magazine

Copy of *Wine Spectator*

Wine bottle stoppers

4 white wineglasses

4 red wineglasses

More Than Basic Basket
(around $50)—add the following

Wine coasters

Wine charms

The Works
($75 to $100)—add the following

Assorted crackers

Gift certificate to local cheese shop

Corkscrew

Cheese knives

Cheese board

Guest's Bedside Basket

A unique gift to deliver to a hotel room, this basket welcomes a client visiting your city or an out-of-towner invited to a wedding or other big event you are hosting. Free tourist brochures are available through your local chamber of commerce or visitors' bureau. If your city is famous for something special, try to gear your choice of souvenirs in that direction. For example, if you are in New York City, include some apples in the basket; in Boston, some Boston baked bean candies; or in Dallas, some Texas-shaped cookies or chips. All the items can be packed into a tote bag that commemorates the event. Getting printed tote bags is simple—your local office supply store can help you.

Basic Basket
(around $25)

Local map with attractions highlighted

Tour tickets to see local attractions

Discount tickets to local attractions

Tokens or passes for public transportation, with schedule and location of nearby stops

Local magazine with week's events listed

Printed note card with important phone numbers and restaurant recommendations

Printed card with schedule of events (for wedding or clients) and directions to each

More Than Basic Basket
(around $50)— add the following

Fresh fruit

Snacks (local specialties or small bags of pretzels, chips, and candy bars)

Bottles of water or sparkling cider

Small guidebook to the area

The Works
(around $75)— add one or more of the following

Bottle of wine

Corkscrew

Disposable cameras

Prepaid calling card

Hearth and Home Basket

This basket makes a great housewarming or hostess gift to bring to friends during the winter. Start with a log carrier as the basket—a brass log holder will work as well as a large canvas one. (The log holder at L.L.Bean is $30, so I start the basic basket at $50.) If you are crafty you can arrange greens on a log with a glue gun for a decorative effect. Otherwise, find a few nice logs to arrange in the basket.

Basic Basket
(around $50)

Fireplace log(s)

Long matches or fireplace lighter

Sticks of kindling tied together with sturdy ribbon

More Than Basic Basket
(around $75)—add one or more of the following

Warm blanket for snuggling

Pinecones dipped in paraffin to add to the fire

Fleece slipper socks

Bottle of brandy

2 snifters

A Bit of Britain Basket

This basket is filled with all things British for friends to enjoy as a housewarming or hostess gift. Although some people may think that all British food is bland, there is nothing bland about a nice curry or a glass of Scotch. A wooden basket will work well here as the container. Fill the bottom with straw, nestle each item into the basket, and cover with cellophane. Decorate with streamer ribbons.

Basic Basket
(around $30)

Tea biscuits or shortbread

Cadbury chocolates (bars are nice)

Assorted English teas

Tea bag caddy

Tea strainer

More Than Basic Basket
(around $60)—add one or more of the following

Teacups and saucers

Pub mats

Bottle of Scotch

The Works
(around $100)—add the following

Teapot or electric kettle

Lump sugar in airtight container

Package of scones or scone mix

Jar of English marmalade

Jar of clotted cream

Jar of chutney

Tin of curry powder

Bottle of HP Sauce

Get Well Basket

When friends are ill or hospitalized, I often send a basket like this to help them pass the time and let them know I'm thinking of them. A traditional basket is always a great choice here, but you could also use a canvas tote bag that they can use to carry things home from the hospital or from room to room.

Basic Basket
(around $25)

Nonalcoholic cider or bottled water

Assorted magazines, rolled and tied with ribbon

Books on audio-cassette or CD

Movie video or DVD

Stuffed teddy bear (comfy companion for any sickbed)

More Than Basic Basket
(around $50)— add the following

Hand lotion

Lip balm

Small packages of tissues

Doodle art poster and felt-tip pens

Pencils

Crossword puzzle book

Thank-you notes with stamps

The Works
(around $100)— add one or more of the following

Warm terry cloth or fleece robe

Portable CD player

Prepaid phone card

Hostess with the Mostest Basket

Whenever we are invited to a friend's house, I try not to bring the same old thing. Giving a bottle of wine doesn't take much imagination, but taking a basket with some special items is usually a hit, and it doesn't cost much more. This basket is simple to put together, and you can go as over the top as you like. Begin with an open wicker basket and add items to coordinate with the season or your host's décor.

Basic Basket
(around $25)

2 packages paper cocktail napkins

2 packages paper hand towels in coordinating pattern or color

2 small votive candles

2 taper candles in coordinating color

Wine charms

More Than Basic Basket
(around $50)— add one or more of the following

Corkscrew

Bottle of wine

Wine coasters

Candleholders

Assistant's Basket

Administrative Professionals Day, the Wednesday of the last full week in April, is the day to recognize the person who is responsible for keeping you organized and looking good. This simple basket is the perfect thing to give to express your appreciation for a job well done. Wrap each item in colored cellophane.

Basic Basket *(around $25)*

Personalized sticky notes

Small picture frame

Letter opener

Hand lotion

Small mirror

Over the Top Basket *(around $150)—add one or more of the following*

Montblanc pen

Small box of chocolates

Gift certificate to local lunch place

Gift certificate to spa for any of the following: facial, manicure, haircut, tanning, or massage

Energy bars

Bottled water

Boss's Retreat Basket

Every boss needs a few things to relieve the stress of the workday, and this is just the basket to do it, especially on October 16, National Boss Day. Pack this assortment into a plastic wastebasket with a big happy face painted on the side.

Basic Basket *(around $25)*

Basketball hoop for wastebasket

Swedish foot massager

Back scratcher

Desk games

Funny sticky notes

More Than Basic Basket *(around $50)— add one or more of the following*

Gift certificate for massage

Energy bars

Funny coffee mug filled with anti-stress vitamins

New Pet Basket

To welcome the newest member of a family, use an animal bed or carrier as your basket, and fill it with pet essentials. Wrap each item in appropriate wrapping paper or tissue paper that you have stamped with black paw prints.

Basic Basket

(since some animal beds are pricey, these baskets begin at around $30)

Small chew toys

Animal treats

Bag of pet food

Pet shampoo

More Than Basic Basket

(around $60)— add the following

Book about pet care

Leash and collar

Personalized animal nametag for collar

Scratching post for a kitten

The Works

($75 to $175)— add the following

Food bowl

Gift certificate to local vet

Gift certificate to local groomer

Copy of James Herriot's *All Creatures Great and Small*

Back to School Basket

This basket is really a backpack that you can gear to the age and grade of the child. I like to start with a really cool backpack in a flowered print for a girl or camouflage for a boy. For the basic basket, skip the backpack and use a box decorated with an appropriate-themed wrapping paper, then add pencils and other items to coordinate with the theme.

Basic Basket

(around $25)

Pencils

Erasers

Erasable pens

Colored pencil set

Crayons

Newsprint pad

Notebook paper (2nd grade and up)

Cool book covers

More Than Basic Basket

(around $50)— add one or more of the following

Backpack

Sticky notes or small memo pads

Stickers

Index cards (3rd grade and up)

Small paint box with brush

Zippered notebook insert for holding pens and pencils

Small calculator

Ruler

Small stapler

Small roll of tape

Thank-you notes

Apple for the Teacher Basket

This "you are appreciated" gift is sure to receive an A+ from the teacher. Start with a shallow rectangular basket or file tray that can become a useful desk accessory for collecting test papers. Playing on the apple theme, fill the basket with the items below. Have your child participate by creating apple-decorated wrapping paper (with crayons and stickers) that goes around the package.

Basic Basket
(around $30)

Red and green pencils

Sticky notes decorated with apples

Teacher's stamps with stamp pads

Bags of apple chips

Apple-flavored jellybeans

2 large red apples

Mug decorated with apples (find one already decorated or buy a plain mug and decorate it with paint pens)

Cinnamon apple tea bags

Got the Munchies Basket

This is the basket for that favorite friend who loves to snack. It could be an "I love you" basket, an attempt to cheer up a friend who's feeling blue, or a congratulations gift. I've also done this as a final exam basket for college students, using a can in the college logo colors or pasting logos onto a plain plastic or metal can with a cover. Layer colored cellophane or tissue in the bottom of the basket or bucket, then wrap it in colored cellophane to give it an upscale look. Make sure to place the heaviest items and those that won't get crushed in the bottom of the basket. Place small candies or packages of chewing gum in a cellophane bag and hang it from the center of the ribbon ties.

Basic Basket
($25 to $50: This is really a mix-and-match proposition. The whole basket will cost about $50, but you can certainly leave some things out.)

Microwave popcorn in assorted flavors

Snack-size bags of tortilla chips

Snack-size bags of potato chips

Jar of salsa

Dip mix

Pretzels

Assorted nuts

Sunflower seeds

Beef jerky

Crackers

Assorted Pepperidge Farm cookies

Snack-size bags of Oreo and Nutter Butter cookies

Jellybeans

Assorted candy bars

Chewing gum or small candies in cellophane bags

Energy bars

More Than Basic Basket
(around $75)— add the following

Gift certificate to local pizza parlor

Beach House Basket

An invitation to spend a day, weekend, or week with friends at their beach house is one that deserves a special basket, and this nautical- or shell-themed basket is just the right gift to bring along for the occasion. Start with a picnic basket or a large canvas tote bag that they can reuse once they empty the contents. Make sure to decorate the basket with shell-themed ribbons, attaching shells to the bottom of each streamer or gluing a large shell to the center of the ribbon.

Basic Basket
(around $30)

Bottle of wine

Crackers or other snacks

Corkscrew

Cocktail napkins

Shell or seascape picture frame

More Than Basic Basket
(around $60)— add one or more of the following

Citronella candles for outdoor entertaining (you can find fun shapes in catalogs or online)

Subscription to *Coastal Living* (or copy of the magazine rolled and tied with ribbon)

Acrylic wineglasses and tray for serving

2 beach towels in shell or nautical theme

Puzzle with beach theme (something to do when the sun goes down)

The Works
(around $120)— add one or more of the following

Tablecloth or place mats and napkins

Gift certificate to local gourmet store (stop there on your way into town) or cheeses and breakfast items for the weekend

Sunblock

Video or DVD boxed set

Pat Conroy's novel *Beach Music*

CDs or gift certificate to Amazon.com

Disposable cameras

Saturday Night at the Movies Basket

This is a terrific basket to take to a friend's house, whether you are going to spend the night or just the evening. Begin with a ceramic or glass popcorn bowl or a container that is shaped like a box of movie popcorn, then fill it with all your favorites. The wire basket shown here makes it convenient to carry all the goodies to the TV room!

Basic Basket
($30 to $50)

Videos or DVDs

Gift certificate to local video store or Amazon.com

Popcorn in assorted flavors

Assorted candies

Paper napkins

Spice mixes or toppings for popcorn

Dental floss

More Than Basic Basket
(around $65)— add the following

Six-pack of soda, with plastic cups and straws

Popcorn popper

DVD storage cube

Après-Ski Basket

Here's another basket to take along on a weekend away with friends, bringing items you'll need to keep warm and snuggly. A basket is especially nice, but you can pack all these items into a nice tote bag, a log holder, or a box that you've decorated yourself.

Basic Basket
(around $30)

Bottle of rum

Hot buttered rum mix

Hot cocoa mix

Candy canes for stirrers

Marshmallows

Hershey's chocolate bars

Package of graham crackers

Long skewers for toasting marshmallows

More Than Basic Basket
(around $60)— add the following

Heatproof glass or ceramic mugs (use ceramic paints to label them with each person's name if you are feeling crafty)

Snacks such as pretzels, chips, and nuts

Bottle of brandy

Jug of apple cider

The Works
(around $100)— add the following

Energy bars

Jars of jam for breakfast

Scone or muffin mix

Granola or muesli for breakfast

Warm, snuggly blanket for cuddling by the fire, or fleece slipper socks for everyone

Disposable hand warmers

Boater's Basket

This is a great gift for friends when you've been invited out on their boat for an afternoon or a weekend. Since boats are small, keep that in mind when filling the basket—everything should be disposable or very small to fit into tight spaces. I like to use a large canvas tote bag that can be reused for carrying things from the car to the boat. Decorate the ribbons with a nautical motif, perhaps gluing small sailboat charms to the streamers or securing a small wooden sailboat (available at a craft store) to the center of the ribbon.

Basic Basket *(around $30)*

Nautical-themed dishes or glassware

Nautical dishtowels

Cocktail napkins

Swiss Army knife with corkscrew

Small wedges of your favorite cheeses (if the basket will be used that day) or gift certificate to local gourmet or cheese shop

Salted or spicy nuts

Crackers in re-sealable airtight containers or tins

Nautical cheese spreaders

Copy of boating magazine

More Than Basic Basket *(around $60)— add one or more of the following*

Hats or visors (name of the boat is a nice touch)

Mugs with logo of the boat or the words "Captain" and "First Mate"

Glasses with logo of the boat

Sunblock

Small first-aid kit

Floatable key chain(s)

Disposable water-proof cameras

Book of day trips for boaters in the area

The Works *(around $125)— add one or more of the following*

T-shirts with logo of the boat or yacht club

Sailboat-shaped picture frame

12-volt battery–powered blender for drinks

Bottle of rum

Bottle of rum punch mix or piña colada mix

Over the Top Basket *(around $500)—add the following*

Hand-held Global Positioning System (GPS) device or gift certificate to local marine supply store

Guy Golfer's Basket

Remember that sports are expensive, so this basket can get pricey fast, but you can find things on the Internet and at your local sporting goods stores on sale to offset the pricier items. You could use a golf shoe bag as the basket, but a canvas tote bag or a paper gift bag from a card shop, maybe with a golf or sports theme, works just as well.

Basic Basket
(around $25)

Golf balls

Golf towel

Golf visor

Golf tees

More Than Basic Basket
(around $60)— add the following

Copy of *Golf Digest*

Sunblock

Energy bars

Gatorade or other sports drink

Club covers

Golf socks

Gift certificate for bucket of balls at the driving range

The Works
($100 to $200)— add the following

Golf shirt (perhaps with logo of favorite course)

Golf hat

Small first-aid kit

Golf glove

Gift certificate for round of golf

Gift certificate for golf lesson(s)

Over the Top Getaway Basket *($250 and up: This basket is for a very special anniversary or birthday present.)— pack a suitcase with the following*

Golf hat or visor with logo of destination

Golf shirt with logo of destination

Gift certificate for round(s) of golf at destination

Golf towel with logo of destination

Golf balls with logo of destination

Airline tickets or map(s) for car trip

Hotel voucher(s) for destination

Itinerary for destination

Bottle of champagne or favorite wine

Lady Golfer's Basket

Pack these items into a tote bag or golf shoe bag, wrapping each one in coordinating colored tissue paper. Or simply arrange your items in a heavy-duty decorated bag from a card or gift store.

Basic Basket
(around $25)

Visor

Golf towel

Golf socks

Sunblock

Lip gloss with sun protection

More Than Basic Basket
(around $60)— add one or more of the following

Copy of *Golf Digest*

Gift certificate for golf lesson(s)

Gift certificate for bucket of balls at the driving range

Small first-aid kit

Sunglasses

The Works
($100 to $150)— add the following

Gift certificate for round of golf

Golf shirt (perhaps with logo of favorite course)

Energy bars

Gatorade or other sports drink

Golf hat

Over the Top Getaway Basket *(see page 47)*

Petite Picasso Basket

A gift to tap into a child's creativity, this basket will keep the youngster busy for hours. Pack these items into a canvas tote bag or plain paper shopping bag that can be decorated with fabric paints or rubber stamps.

Basic Basket
(around $30)

Colored pens and pencils

Doodle art poster

Stencils

Large newsprint pad

Painting smock

More Than Basic Basket
(around $50)— add the following

Puffy paints

Fabric paints

Fabric crayons

White cotton hat to paint

T-shirt to decorate

The Works
(around $75)— add the following

Glue

Package of felt squares

Yarn

Package of beads

Lap desk

Sports Fan Basket

My son, Ryan, is a sports fanatic. He loves to play sports, but he also loves to watch and report on sports. This is his idea of the perfect gift for the sports fan. Use a plastic can with a lid (in the colors of the person's favorite team, if possible). Or decorate the outside of the can with sports logos. For the basic basket, you could use the cooler as the container.

Basic Basket
(around $25)

Small soft-sided insulated cooler for drinks

Insulated mug with favorite team's logo

Cap with favorite team's logo

More Than Basic Basket
(around $50)— add the following

Team pennant

Large bag of peanuts

Nerf basketball with net or football

Wiffle ball and bat set

The Works
($100 and up)— add one or more of the following

Tickets to an upcoming game

Sports almanac

Team shirt

Gift certificate to local sporting goods store

Issue of *Sporting News* or *Sports Illustrated*

Tennis Basket

This basket could be a canvas tote bag, a tennis bag, or a backpack, depending on your budget. It should contain lots of fun things for your favorite tennis player. If the recipient is a novice, you might want to include tennis lessons, too.

Basic Basket
(around $30)

Tennis balls

Ball holder

Visor or hat

Small first-aid kit

More Than Basic Basket
(around $60)— add the following

Wristbands

Sunblock

Lip balm

Socks

Scorekeeper that hangs over net

Copy of *Tennis* magazine rolled and tied with ribbon

The Works
(around $100)— add one or more of the following

Tennis bag

Subscription to *Tennis* magazine

Gift certificate for tennis lesson, or lessons on video or DVD

Book about tennis

Fun and Games Basket

One Thanksgiving we were invited to a friend's home for dinner and to spend the night. Since all ages were represented, we brought a basket of games and puzzles and spent the evening playing games and doing puzzles together. This basket is best wrapped as a tower, stacked from largest box to smallest, with the largest on the bottom. Wrap the entire thing in cellophane. If you are giving only a few small games or puzzles, a basket works fine. A large plastic tub with a top also works well and can be reused for storage. This makes a great housewarming gift or hostess gift at the holidays. It's also a terrific family gift for the holidays, instead of buying individual presents. Feel free to substitute your favorite games for the ones suggested here. I find that the classics bring out the kid in everyone.

Basic Basket
(around $30)

Scrabble

Monopoly

Candy Land (if smaller children are included)

500-piece jigsaw puzzle (holiday theme for Christmas, autumn scene for Thanksgiving, or ocean scene for friends who have a beach house, for example)

2 decks of cards

More Than Basic Basket
(around $60)— add the following

Crossword puzzle games

Puzzles for smaller children or an additional puzzle

Life

Yahtzee

Poker chips

The Works
(around $100)— add the following

Checkers and chess in travel package

Jenga wooden puzzle

Additional puzzles

Magic Eye book of puzzles

Boggle

Trivial Pursuit

Jeopardy!

Gardener's Helper Basket

This gardening basket is for a friend who loves his or her garden. You can also make it into a children's basket by adjusting the contents for a child's garden and putting everything into a colorful plastic box. A classic basket is a great choice for a container, but you can also use a plastic box or tote bag for this gift. If you want to give the $25 gift, a four-inch unglazed flowerpot makes a charming container. For the works, use the cart as the container.

Basic Basket
(around $25)

Garden shears

Spade

Hand rake

Garden gloves

More Than Basic Basket
(around $50)— add the following

Kneeling pad

Misting bottle

Seeds for vegetables and herbs, or small plants

Garden ornament

The Works
(over $100)—add the following

Rolling garden cart

Gardening book(s)

Gift certificate to nursery

Basket for Children
($25 to $30)

Children's gardening book

Seeds for flowers or vegetables

Seedling pots to plant the seeds in

Garden gloves

Small, nonpointed spade for digging

Misting bottle

Bird Watcher's Basket

Any bird watcher will love this basket filled with items for his or her favorite hobby. A wooden basket works beautifully, or you can use a nice backpack that the recipient can use to carry all the essentials for a day of bird watching.

Basic Basket
(around $30)

Bird watcher's book of local birds

Sunblock

Hat

Bird feeder

Birdseed

More Than Basic Basket
(around $60)— add one or more of the following

Binoculars

CD of birdcalls

Hummingbird feeder

Disposable cameras

Writing Desk Basket

This basket is a nice desktop center made of either Lucite or wood, which is then packed with all the essentials needed to write notes and letters. It is an especially nice gift for a bride-to-be, who will be writing endless thank-you notes, or for a friend who simply enjoys writing. Start with a desktop organizer set inside a rectangular basket filled with cellophane or straw, then add the other items, covering the entire basket with cellophane and decorating it with streamer ribbons. Office supply stores are treasure-troves of supplies for this basket.

Basic Basket
(around $25)

Assorted pens (be creative and buy different types, such as rolling ball and ballpoint in assorted colors; think silver and gold specialty pens for glamorous invitations)

Assorted pencils

Assorted notepads (for shopping lists, phone messages, and scribbling)

Sticky notes

Small stapler

Small roll of tape

Small scissors

Note cards for thank-you notes and short letters

Attractive postage stamps

More Than Basic Basket
(around $50)— add the following

Calligraphy set

Nice linen stationery

Personalized return address labels

The Works
(around $100)— add the following

Rubber stamps

Embosser for return address

Personalized stationery

Stickers for decorating letters and notes

Initial seal with wax

Fiesta Basket

Since I live in California, this is my first choice for a basket when I'm going to someone's home. Festive and filled with all the ingredients necessary for a Mexican fiesta, it's a winner anytime, anywhere. Begin with a large, rustic-looking basket and fill it with your favorite goodies.

Basic Basket
(around $30)

Serape or colorful tablecloth

Gold tequila

Coarse salt

Margarita mix

Fresh limes

Fresh avocados

More Than Basic Basket
(around $60)— add the following

Assorted dried chiles

Assorted chili powders

Margarita pitcher

Margarita glasses

The Works
(around $100)— add the following

Small chip and dip set

Jar of salsa

Assorted tortilla chips

Jar of hot pickled vegetables

Southwestern cookbook

Well-Stocked Pot Basket

Soups and stews are some of my favorite foods, and this basket makes a great gift for a wedding shower or house-warming. Begin with a stockpot or Dutch oven and fill it with all the things necessary to make a terrific soup or stew. If this gift is for a wedding, I recommend that you check the bride's registry to see which brands she is registered for and buy her one of those, rather than make that choice yourself. I find that discount housewares stores have stockpots and Dutch ovens at reasonable prices, but the pot itself is the most expensive part of the basket. If you would rather give the other items and keep it less expensive, use a nice basket instead.

Basic Basket
(around $30 with basket)

Gourmet soup mix or soup base

Ladle

Soup bowls or mugs

Potholders

Apron

More Than Basic Basket
(around $60 with stockpot)—add the following

Pepper mill with peppercorns

Heatproof spatula

Martini Basket

This sophisticated basket could be a housewarming present, a gift for the boss, or a nice wedding shower gift. Pack everything into a basket that you have spray-painted silver and filled with straw. Cover it with clear cellophane and add black and white streamer ribbons to give this basket nice clean lines.

Basic Basket
(around $30)

Stainless steel cocktail shaker

2 martini glasses

Cocktail strainer

More Than Basic Basket
(around $50)— add the following

Fancy toothpicks for olives

Assorted stuffed olives (look for those stuffed with onions, garlic, jalapeños, and even almonds or orange peel)

Glass swizzle sticks

Book on martinis

The Works
(around $100)— add the following

Serving tray

Bottle of vodka or gin

Bottle of dry vermouth

Additional martini glasses

Over the Top Basket *(around $150)—add the following*

Stainless steel ice bucket with insulated liner

Well-Stocked Bar Basket

This basket is for someone who is setting up a new home or whose bar is in need of some sprucing up. You can give all the essentials needed for a portable party to a host or hostess or to a newly married couple. Start with a nice picnic basket lined with a table runner that can double as a bar cloth, or use an ice bucket and fill it with small items. Decorate the basket with streamer ribbons, attaching swizzle sticks to the ribbons.

Basic Basket
(around $25)

Corkscrew

Bottle opener

Shot glass

Cocktail strainer

Long-handled spoon for stirring

Swizzle sticks

Decorative picks for skewering garnishes

Cloth or humorous paper cocktail napkins

More Than Basic Basket
(around $50)— add one or more of the following

Ice bucket

Cocktail shaker

Bar mop towels

Small cutting board

Bartender's guide

6- and 8-ounce tumblers

Jar of maraschino cherries

Jar of olives

Jar of pickled onions

The Works
(around $100)— add the following

Bottle of gin, vodka, tequila, Scotch, and/or bourbon

Slow Cooker Basket

This is another winner for a wedding shower, anniversary, or special birthday. Slow cookers have come a long way, and they range in price from about $25 to more than $100. Since the basket here is the slow cooker, the Basic Basket is a bit over our $25 to $30 average. Wrap the slow cooker in cellophane and tie it with streamer ribbons, crossing two wooden spoons through the center of the ribbon knot.

Basic Basket
(around $40)

Ladle

Potholders

More Than Basic Basket
(around $60)— add one or more of the following

Heatproof spatula

Wooden spoon

Matching dishtowels

Basic slow cooker cookbook

Clambake Basket

Having grown up in New England, I think there's nothing better on a summer afternoon than steamed lobsters with all the fixings. You can get your friends ready for that clambake by giving them this basket filled with all the tools needed to cook and eat lobsters, clams, and your favorite accouterments. Use a traditional enamelware lobster pot for the basket, then fill it with goodies. Tie the whole thing up with cellophane and streamer ribbons.

Basic Basket
(around $30)

Nutcrackers

Picks for digging out lobster meat (sold with the nutcrackers)

Red-and-white-checked paper tablecloth

Red-and-white-checked paper napkins

Lobster bibs

More Than Basic Basket
(around $50)— add the following

Large ceramic bowl for discarded shells

Small glass or metal bowls for melted butter

Fresh lemons

Cheesecloth to wrap the cut lemons

Tongs for lifting out the lobsters

The Works
(around $100)— add the following

Gift certificate for lobsters from local purveyor or MaineLobsterDirect.com

---

Picnic Basket

Children and adults will love this alfresco basket, packed with all they need to have a picnic in the park or on the back patio. Line a lidded picnic hamper with a 40-inch square tablecloth and four matching napkins. Coordinate lightweight acrylic tableware available in a range of festive colors.

Basic Basket
(around $30)

4 acrylic wineglasses

4 acrylic plates

4 lightweight place settings of flatware, plus 2 serving spoons

More Than Basic Basket
(around $60)— add one or more of the following

4 acrylic dessert bowls

4 napkin rings

4 insulated acrylic mugs

Thermos

The Works
($100 to $125)— add the following

Plastic food containers

Acrylic saltshaker and pepper mill

Bottle of wine

Corkscrew

Gift certificate to local gourmet market

Little Red Wagon

I have always loved the Radio Flyer red wagon, and this basket is actually a Radio Flyer filled with something for the entire family. It's a bit over the top in terms of price, but it's such a nice gift that I wanted to include it. You could also buy the smaller, desk-size Radio Flyer and fill it with candy and other items if you'd like to give a small gift.

Over the Top Basket *(around $100)*

Blanket or throw to line the wagon

Radio Flyer hats for the whole family

Teddy bears for the children

Puzzles or board games of your choice

Decks of cards

Popcorn in assorted flavors

Guest's Bath Basket

A welcome gift for overnight guests, this basket contains all the things they might forget to bring. Use a round basket with a handle, line it with four washcloths, and fill it with grooming essentials.

Basic Basket *(around $25)*

4 washcloths

Sample sizes of shampoo and conditioner

Assorted soaps (deodorant and facial)

Sample size of deodorant

Shower cap

Moisturizing lotion

Lint brush

Dusting powder

Disposable razor

Shaving cream

Toothpaste

Toothbrush

Dental floss

Adhesive bandages

Cotton swabs

Cotton balls for makeup removal

Sample sizes of aspirin, acetaminophen, and ibuprofen

Sample sizes of stomach remedies

Small bottles of water

More Than Basic Basket *($50 to $75)—add the following*

Folded kimono, tied with ribbon

Disposable paper slippers

Current magazine, tied with ribbon

Taste of the Tropics Basket

This is the quintessential tropical hangout basket. Whether you give this to a friend who's celebrating a milestone, take it along for a weekend at the beach, or simply decide that it's time for a little bit of the tropics in the dead of winter, this basket has all the makings for a great time. A basket would be my choice here to hold all these fun things. Wrap each separately in tissue or cellophane, then wrap the entire basket in colored cellophane, using streamer ribbons or crepe paper rolls.

Basic Basket
(around $30)

- Bottle of rum
- Bottle of piña colada mix
- Macadamia nuts
- Fresh pineapple
- Tropical-themed cocktail napkins
- Paper umbrellas for drinks

More Than Basic Basket
(around $60)— add the following

- 8-ounce acrylic tropical-themed glasses
- Tropical-themed coasters
- Tiki candles or other tropical candles ("plant" candles that look like lollipops and have a tropical theme in a glass vase filled with sand)

The Works
($100 to $150)— add the following

- CD of island music
- Portable CD player
- Blender for drinks
- Plastic inflatable palm tree (available through Off the Deep End; see Source Guide)
- Plastic inflatable flamingos
- Caribbean cookbook

Festival Italiano Basket

Being of Italian descent, I love just about anything to do with Italy and sharing that love with others. Just line the basket with a pretty tablecloth or napkins and fill it up. On several occasions, I have used a red-and-white-checked tablecloth to wrap this basket. I tie coordinating napkins together and use them as the ribbon ties, inserting a wooden spoon in the center of the tie.

Basic Basket
(around $25)

Extra-virgin olive oil

Balsamic vinegar

Dried Italian herbs (oregano, basil, rosemary)

Red pepper flakes

Imported pasta in different shapes

Marinated artichoke hearts

Perugina chocolates

More Than Basic Basket
(around $50)—add the following

Sun-dried tomatoes packed in olive oil

Giardiniera (pickled vegetable medley)

Dried porcini mushrooms

Truffle paste

Illy coffee or espresso

Amaretti and biscotti (cookies)

The Works
(around $100)—add one or more of the following

Bottle of Italian red wine

Bottle of Prosecco

Bottle of limoncello

Gift certificate to local Italian grocery store or restaurant

Italian cookbook

Chunk of Parmigiano-Reggiano cheese

Tool Time Basket

This is a nice gift for someone moving into his or her first home or apartment. A fishing tackle box is fitted out with all the essentials for hanging pictures and doing odd jobs around the house. If you want to go way over the top, buy a tool chest and fill it with tools. My husband is nick-named Dr. Fix-It because he can fix just about anything, and he recommends Craftsman tools from Sears. He says that you really do get what you pay for with tools, and he recommends buying the best you can afford.

Basic Basket
(around $30)

Hammer

Screwdriver with multiple heads

Pliers

Wire cutters

Scissors

Picture hangers

Picture frame wire

Nails

Basic do-it-yourself book

More Than Basic Basket
(around $50)— add the following

Channel lock pliers (great for kitchen faucets)

Glue gun

Sandpaper blocks

White glue

Tape measure

Can of WD-40

Small tube of silicone caulking (type that doesn't need gun)

The Works
(around $100)— add the following

Electric drill

FOOD BASKETS

Cookie Monster's Basket

Cut-Out Cookie Basket

Sweetheart Basket

Cookie Lover's Basket

Loaf of Bread Basket

Bed and Breakfast Tray

Weekend Breakfast Basket

Lettuce Entertain You Basket

Presto Pesto Basket

Flavored Vinegar Basket

Soup's On Basket

Luck of the Irish Basket

Lone Star Chili Basket

Tea for Two Basket

Great Grains Basket

Bistro Basket

Trattoria Basket

Cinco de Mayo Basket

Mardi Gras Basket

Chocoholic's Basket

Let Them Eat Cake Basket

Sundae Best Basket

Wok on the Wild Side Basket

Make Lemonade Basket

Grillin' and Chillin' Basket

Coffee Aficionado's Basket

Hooray for the Red, White, and Blue Basket

Pizza Pizzazz Basket

Spooky Halloween Basket

Gingerbread House Basket

Thanksgiving Basket

Happy Hanukkah Basket

Ring in the New Year Basket

Gifts of food are always appreciated. Whether it's a basket of homemade cookies or a bundt pan filled with cake mixes, a food gift is sure to bring a smile to the face of anyone who receives it. When I first began giving gift mixes, I would make up mixes and fill cellophane bags or vacuum-sealed jars and give them along with the recipe for making the mix. Sometimes I would add a cooking implement: a ladle with a soup mix, a spatula or offset spatula with a cake mix, a chocolate spoon with a drink mix. For more elaborate gifts, I would give a "meal kit": dip, drink, soup, bread, and dessert mixes, with recipes attached, all placed in a basket or other container based on the flavors and theme of the meal. My friends loved receiving these containers and being able to put together something special from the mixes.

The variety of containers you have to choose from is vast, and your choice depends on what you can afford and how over the top you want to go. Soup tureens, salad spinners, salad bowls, stockpots, cookie jars, teapots, ice buckets, water pitchers, colanders, canisters, and baskets of infinite variety all make useful containers for culinary gifts. If economy is a priority, try recycling interesting jars. Cover the tops with seasonal fabric that has been cut with pinking shears (no frayed ends) and tie with ribbon or raffia. Or use pinking shears to cut long strips of fabric for ribbon ties.

To ready recycled jars for filling, wash them in warm soapy water, then soak off the labels. If the labels are particularly stubborn, use a liquid solvent such as Goo Gone, WD-40, or De-Solv-It. Cellophane bags are available in most floral supply stores, or you can find decorative bags at gourmet retailers. Plain old plastic food storage bags without the zipper top also can be used; just make sure to use pretty ribbon or raffia ties to dress them up. White and brown lunch bags can be decorated with stickers or rubber stamps and used for less expensive gifts or for party favors.

Each food basket in this chapter includes something to make—either a mix and accompanying recipe or a baked item and gift tag. At your local copy center, you can copy the recipe instructions on colored or plain white card stock and give this along with the gift. If you are particularly skilled at crafting, copy the recipes longhand and decorate them with rubber stamps or stickers. This is your basket; personalize it to make it your own.

When choosing foods for your basket, make sure they are fresh and shelf stable. Herbs for mixes should be dried and whole, not rubbed or ground, unless indicated in the recipes. Herbs lose most of their essential oils when they are rubbed or ground. Vacuum-packed salami that can be stored at room temperature can be used in a basket, but I would avoid fresh meats and cheeses unless the basket will be consumed as soon as it's given. The same holds true for fresh fruits and veggies: make sure your recipient will use them within a short period of time. When you arrive with the basket, you might say, "If you aren't going to use these items right away, we should refrigerate them."

Cookie Monster's Basket

I don't know anyone who doesn't like cookies, and this basket provides some creative inspiration. I love to pack these mixes with the ingredients layered in jars, then nest them in a basket along with silicone baking mats, a cookie scoop, heatproof spatulas, and the recipes. This is a terrific gift for a young adult in a first apartment or for your favorite family at holiday time. The mixes also can be given individually as smaller gifts, either layered in jars or combined in cellophane bags. Use them as hostess gifts or party favors.

Candy Cookie Mix

Makes about 3 cups

This versatile cookie mix lends itself to imaginative creations using various candies, such as Reese's Peanut Butter Cups or Butterfinger bars. Include a small bag of the appropriate candy in the basket. I like to layer the ingredients in a 3 1/2-cup jar.

2 cups all-purpose flour
1/2 cup firmly packed light brown sugar
1/2 cup granulated sugar
1 teaspoon vanilla powder
1 teaspoon baking soda

In a medium-size bowl, combine the ingredients and store in an airtight container. Or layer the ingredients in an attractive jar. Label with a 3-month expiration date.

Oatmeal Chocolate Chippers Mix

Makes about 9 1/3 cups

This mix is really nice to layer in a jar, but you can certainly blend the ingredients together and store the mix in your favorite airtight container.

1 cup firmly packed light brown sugar
3/4 cup granulated sugar
1 1/2 cups old-fashioned rolled oats

2 cups semisweet or milk chocolate chips
2 cups all-purpose flour
1 teaspoon baking soda
2 teaspoons vanilla powder
2 cups chopped pecans or walnuts

In a large bowl, combine the ingredients and store in an airtight container. Or layer the ingredients in an attractive jar. Label with a 3-month expiration date.

Fudge Brownie Mound Cookie Mix

Makes about 7 3/4 cups

3 1/3 cups all-purpose flour
1 teaspoon baking powder
1/2 teaspoon salt
1 1/2 cups sugar
1 1/4 cups cocoa powder
1 tablespoon vanilla powder
1 1/2 cups chopped walnuts or pecans

In a large bowl, combine the ingredients and store in an airtight container. Or layer the ingredients in an attractive jar. Label with a 1-month expiration date.

Candy Cookies

Makes about 3 dozen cookies

1 cup (2 sticks) unsalted butter
1 large egg
1 package Candy Cookie Mix

1 cup candy chunks (Reese's Peanut Butter Cups, Butterfinger bars, M&M's, Heath bars, or white or semisweet chocolate chunks)

1. Preheat the oven to 350°F. Line baking sheets with silicone baking mats, parchment paper, or aluminum foil. In a large bowl using an electric mixer, beat the butter until smooth. Add the egg and continue beating until combined. Add the Candy Cookie Mix and candy chunks and blend on low until the cookie mix is just incorporated.

2. Scoop the batter with a 1-inch ice cream scoop or shape it into golf ball–size balls. Place 2 inches apart on the prepared baking sheets. Wet your hands and flatten the cookies so they are 1/2 inch thick. Bake for 10 to 12 minutes, until golden on the edges. Remove from the oven, let cool for 2 minutes, and transfer to a wire rack to cool completely. The cookies will keep in an airtight container at room temperature for up to 3 days or in the freezer for up to 2 months.

Oatmeal Chocolate Chippers

Makes about 3 dozen cookies

1 package Oatmeal Chocolate Chippers Mix

1 cup (2 sticks) unsalted butter, softened
2 large eggs

1. Preheat the oven to 350°F and line baking sheets with silicone baking mats, parchment paper, or aluminum foil. In a large bowl using an electric mixer, blend the Oatmeal Chocolate Chippers Mix with the butter and eggs until combined.

2. Roll the dough into golf ball–size pieces and place on the prepared baking sheets, 1 1/2 inches apart. Wet your hands and flatten the cookies to 3/4 inch thick. Bake for 9 to 12 minutes, until golden on the edges. Remove from the oven and let cool on the baking sheets for 10 minutes. Transfer to a wire rack to cool completely. The cookies will keep in an airtight container for up to 4 days.

Fudge Brownie Mound Cookies

Makes about 4 dozen cookies

1 package Fudge Brownie Mound Cookie Mix
3/4 cup (1 1/2 sticks) unsalted butter, melted

2/3 cup light corn syrup
2 large eggs

1. Preheat the oven to 350°F. Line baking sheets with silicone baking mats, aluminum foil, or parchment paper. In a large bowl using an electric mixer, combine the Fudge Brownie Mound Cookie Mix, butter, corn syrup, and eggs until blended. The mixture will be stiff.

2. Scoop or shape the batter into golf ball–size balls. Place on the prepared baking sheets. Bake for 8 to 10 minutes, until set. Remove from the oven and cool on the baking sheets for 2 minutes, then transfer to wire racks to cool completely. The cookies will keep in an airtight container for up to 4 days.

Cut-Out Cookie Basket

Children love to play in the kitchen. Whether rolling out Play-Doh, making cookies with Mom, or filling the sink with soapy water to wash dishes, they enjoy playing grown-up. And there is nothing more satisfying for younger chefs than taking a few ingredients and turning them into something everyone will love to eat.

This basket is geared toward children ages four to eight, but you could easily tailor it for an older child by choosing different cookie cutters and decorating paints. I don't know anyone who doesn't love cookies, and this basket is sure to be a winner when you give it to that budding chef.

The container could be a colorful plastic box that can be used later for toys or art projects. Other container options include a tool kit or a Jelly-type handbag. Pack the cookie mixes with cookie cutters, a silicone spatula, decorative sprinkles, cake decorating tubes in assorted colors, chocolate chips, a small rolling pin, a child-size apron, and a potholder. Don't forget a paper or cloth chef's hat, which you can purchase at a gourmet retail store or through the mail. Tailor the basket to the season, lining it with seasonal fabric and including appropriate cookie cutters, such as orange and black fabric with pumpkin and witch cookie cutters for Halloween, or red and white fabric with heart-shaped cookie cutters for Valentine's Day.

For a more economical gift, buy white paper lunch bags, decorate them with rubber stamps, and include just the cookie mixes and cutters. The cookie mixes also make unique party favors packed in cellophane bags with a seasonal cookie cutter attached to each.

Ginger Person Cookie Mix

Makes about 2 1/2 cups

The spicy aroma of gingerbread cookies is always welcome in the kitchen, and it's fun to decorate them.

1/2 cup firmly packed dark brown sugar
2 cups all-purpose flour
1 1/4 teaspoons ground ginger
3/4 teaspoon ground cinnamon
1/2 teaspoon baking soda

In a medium-size bowl, combine the ingredients. Store in an airtight container and label with a 3-month expiration date.

Favorite Sugar Cookie Mix

Makes a little more than 4 1/3 cups

1 1/3 cups sugar
2 tablespoons vanilla powder
3 cups all-purpose flour
1/2 teaspoon baking soda
1 teaspoon cream of tartar

In a medium-size bowl, combine the ingredients. Store in an airtight container and label with a 3-month expiration date.

Ginger Person Cookies

Makes about 2 dozen cookies

1/2 cup (1 stick) unsalted butter, softened

1/4 cup dark molasses

1 large egg

1 package Ginger Person Cookie Mix

All-purpose flour for rolling cookies

1. In a large bowl using an electric mixer, cream the butter. Add the molasses and egg, beating until well combined. Beat in the Ginger Person Cookie Mix and mix until blended; the dough should be stiff.

2. Divide the dough in half and flatten each half into a 1-inch-thick round. Wrap in plastic and refrigerate for 2 hours.

3. Preheat the oven to 350°F. Line baking sheets with silicone baking mats, parchment paper, or aluminum foil. Roll the dough out on a lightly floured board to a 1/4-inch thickness. Cut into shapes using floured cookie cutters. Place the cookies 1 inch apart on the prepared baking sheets. Bake for about 12 minutes, until the edges are lightly browned. Let cool for 2 minutes on the baking sheets, then transfer to a wire rack to cool completely. When the cookies are cooled, decorate or frost. They will keep in an airtight container for up to 4 days.

Favorite Sugar Cookies

Makes about 3 dozen cookies

1 package Favorite Sugar Cookie Mix

1 1/2 cups (3 sticks) unsalted butter, softened

2 large eggs

Confectioners' sugar

1/4 cup milk, or as needed

Colored sugar

1. In a large bowl using an electric mixer, blend the Favorite Sugar Cookie Mix, butter, and eggs until the dough begins to come together. Turn the dough out onto a large piece of plastic wrap and form into a rectangle about 1/2 inch thick. Wrap in plastic and refrigerate for at least 1 hour.

2. Preheat the oven to 375°F. Line baking sheets with silicone baking mats, parchment paper, or aluminum foil. Sift confectioners' sugar over the work surface and roll out the dough to a 1/4-inch thickness. Cut into the desired shapes and transfer to the prepared baking sheets using a thin spatula. Brush the cookies with milk and sprinkle with colored sugar. Bake for 10 to 12 minutes, until lightly browned around the edges. Let cool on the baking sheets for 3 to 4 minutes before transferring to a wire rack to cool completely. The cookies will keep in an airtight container for up to 3 days or in the freezer for up to 2 months.

Sweetheart Basket

Fresh strawberries, Belgian Waffle Mix, a heart-shaped waffle iron, and a jug of pure maple syrup, all packed into a white basket trimmed with red dishtowels or a tablecloth and napkins, make the perfect gift for Valentine's Day or whenever you want to say "You're a sweetheart!" to someone who's done something wonderful for you. A friend gave this as a holiday gift to her entire family, and it was their favorite present. After unwrapping all their other gifts, they made the waffles and enjoyed a great breakfast. Fill out the basket with fresh oranges for juice and a spiral-sliced ham to serve alongside the waffles.

Belgian Waffle Mix

Makes about 2 1/4 cups

Fill an old-fashioned canning jar with the mix and top with a red-and-white-print fabric, or decorate the jar with heart stickers.

2 cups all-purpose flour
1 teaspoon salt
1 tablespoon baking powder
1 tablespoon vanilla powder

In a medium-size bowl, combine the ingredients. Store in an airtight container and label with a 3-month expiration date.

Belgian Waffles   *Serves 2 to 4*

3 large eggs, separated
2 tablespoons unsalted butter, melted
1 cup milk
1 cup plus 2 tablespoons Belgian Waffle Mix

Warm maple syrup for serving
Fresh strawberries and whipped cream for serving

Preheat a waffle iron. In a small bowl using an electric mixer, beat the egg whites to soft peaks and set aside. In another bowl, combine the egg yolks, butter, and milk. Whisk in the Belgian Waffle Mix and fold in the egg whites with a wire whisk. Cook according to the waffle iron manufacturer's directions. Serve immediately with maple syrup and/or fresh strawberries and whipped cream.

Cookie Lover's Basket

A basket of freshly baked cookies says "I love you." These are the cookies I make when I want to put together a love basket for a good friend. Whether you make one variety or all of them, your basket will be filled with delicious treats. You can pack your cookies in a cookie jar or other interesting container, such as an earthenware bean crock, a wide-mouthed teapot, or a metal milk pail. Line the container with cellophane and arrange the cookies inside. Then decorate the top with colored streamer ribbons. Don't forget to share the recipes with your friend.

Mrs. Phillips's White Chocolate Macadamia Nut Wonders

Makes about 4 dozen cookies

These cookies will remind you of the ones sold at upscale bakeries, except for the price.

1 cup (2 sticks) unsalted butter, softened

1 cup firmly packed light brown sugar

3/4 cup granulated sugar

2 large eggs

2 teaspoons vanilla extract

2 1/4 cups all-purpose flour

1 teaspoon baking soda

1 teaspoon salt

2 cups white chocolate chips, or 12 ounces white chocolate, coarsely chopped

2 cups chopped macadamia nuts

1 1/2 cups unsweetened flaked coconut

1. Preheat the oven to 350° F. Line baking sheets with silicone baking mats, parchment paper, or aluminum foil. In a large bowl using an electric mixer, cream together the butter and sugars. Add the eggs and vanilla and blend until smooth. Add the flour, baking soda, salt, chocolate chips, nuts, and coconut and mix until just blended.

2. Roll the dough into 1-inch balls and place 1 1/2 inches apart on the prepared baking sheets. Bake for 9 to 12 minutes, until light golden brown. Transfer to a wire rack to cool. The cookies will keep in an airtight container for up to 3 days or in the freezer for up to 2 months.

Amaretto Shortbread

Makes about 5 dozen cookies

This distinctive shortbread with crunchy almonds adds a nice touch to a basket of assorted cookies.

1 cup (2 sticks) cold unsalted
    butter, cut into $1/2$-inch pieces
1 cup plus 2 tablespoons sugar
1 large egg, separated

$1/4$ cup amaretto
2 cups all-purpose flour
$2/3$ cup sliced almonds

1. Preheat the oven to 325°F. Line a 15 x $10^{1}/_{2}$-inch jellyroll pan with a silicone baking mat, aluminum foil, or parchment paper. In a medium-size bowl, cut the butter into the 1 cup sugar. Add the egg yolk and 3 tablespoons of the amaretto. Stir in the flour until well blended and transfer to the prepared pan, using a piece of plastic wrap to pat the dough into place.

2. Beat the egg white with the remaining 1 tablespoon amaretto and brush the dough evenly with the mixture. Distribute the almonds over the top of the shortbread and sprinkle the remaining 2 tablespoons sugar over the almonds. Bake for 40 minutes, or until the shortbread is golden. Cut into 1-inch squares while still warm. The cookies will keep in an airtight container for up to 4 days or in the freezer for up to 2 months.

Double Chocolate Chunk Cookies

Makes about 4 dozen cookies

These rich cookies are soft and chewy, with a bold cocoa flavor and smooth, sweet white chocolate chips. They are sophisticated but so homey. Plan to make a double batch, because they'll go quickly!

$1^{1}/_{2}$ cups (3 sticks) unsalted butter
$1/2$ cup firmly packed light brown
    sugar
$1/2$ cup granulated sugar
3 teaspoons vanilla extract
2 large eggs
$1/2$ teaspoon baking soda

$1/2$ teaspoon salt
1 cup Dutch process cocoa
$3^{1}/_{2}$ cups all-purpose flour
2 cups white chocolate chips, or
    12 ounces white chocolate,
    coarsely chopped

1. Preheat the oven to 350°F. Line baking sheets with silicone baking mats, parchment paper, or aluminum foil. In a large bowl using an electric mixer, cream the butter and sugars until fluffy. Mix in the vanilla and eggs (the mixture should look curdled). Slowly add the baking soda, salt, cocoa, flour, and chocolate chips, beating until the flour disappears.

2. Drop full tablespoons of the mixture 2 inches apart on the prepared baking sheets. Bake for 10 to 12 minutes, until the edges are firm but the middles still look soft. Remove from the oven and let cool on the baking sheets for 3 minutes. Transfer to wire racks to cool completely. The cookies will keep in an airtight container for up to 3 days or in the freezer for up to 2 months.

Loaf of Bread Basket

Deliciously different bread mixes make this basket a terrific wedding shower or housewarming present. Give these mixes in a large earthenware bowl that can be used for mixing the dough, and include a serrated knife and cutting board. Or line a long breadbasket with a colorful napkin and nestle in the mixes. You could even buy a breadbox and fill it with the bread mixes, jams (homemade or store-bought), a serrated knife, and a breadboard. For a small gift, pack the bread mixes in cellophane bags, glass jars, or vacuum jars, wrap in a pretty dishtowel, tie with twine or raffia, and attach the recipes and a spatula for mixing.

Old-Fashioned Herbed Oatmeal Bread Mix

Makes about 5 1/2 cups

1 package active dry yeast
1/2 cup old-fashioned rolled oats
3 tablespoons powdered buttermilk
1 tablespoon sugar
1 teaspoon dillweed
1/2 teaspoon dried thyme
1/2 teaspoon dried sage
1 cup whole wheat flour
4 cups all-purpose flour
1 1/2 teaspoons salt

In a large bowl, combine the ingredients. Store in an airtight container and label with a 3-month expiration date.

Cornmeal and Molasses Bread Mix

Makes about 4 cups

This bread reminds me of those that my grandmother baked when we visited her in New England.

1/2 cup stone-ground yellow cornmeal
2 teaspoons salt

1 package active dry yeast
3 1/2 cups all-purpose flour
1/2 cup whole wheat flour

In a medium-size bowl, combine the ingredients. Store in an airtight container and label with a 3-month expiration date.

Simply Sensational Beer Bread Mix

Makes about 3 cups

This is an economical bread mix to give to friends. Try adding a couple of tablespoons of your favorite herbs for herbed beer bread, or a teaspoon of chipotle chili powder for some smoky heat.

3 cups self-rising flour
3 tablespoons sugar

In a medium-size bowl, combine the ingredients. Store in an airtight container and label with a 3-month expiration date.

Old-Fashioned Herbed Oatmeal Bread

Makes 2 loaves

1 package Old-Fashioned Herbed
Oatmeal Bread Mix

3/4 cup lukewarm water
(105° to 115°F)

1 1/4 cups milk

1 large egg

All-purpose flour, if needed

2 tablespoons unsalted butter,
melted

1. In a large bowl using an electric mixer, blend the Old-Fashioned Herbed Oatmeal Bread Mix with the water and milk and begin to mix with a dough hook. Add the egg and continue to beat until the mixture comes away from the sides of the bowl and forms a ball. If the dough is too sticky, add 2 tablespoons flour and continue to beat, adding more flour if needed. If the dough is too dry, add about a tablespoon of water, adding more if needed.

2. Turn the dough out onto a floured board and knead for 5 minutes, until shiny and elastic. Place the dough in an oiled bowl, turning to coat. Let rise for about 1 hour, until doubled in bulk. Punch the dough down and divide in half. Form each half into an 8-inch loaf and place in an oiled loaf pan. Or shape each half into a round and place on an oiled baking sheet. Cover and let rise for 45 minutes, until doubled in bulk.

3. Preheat the oven to 350°F. Brush the loaves with the butter and bake for 35 to 45 minutes, until they sound hollow when tapped and are golden brown. Place the pans on wire racks and let cool for 30 minutes. Remove the loaves from the pans and let cool completely. The bread will keep, wrapped in plastic, at room temperature for up to 2 days or in the freezer for up to 1 month.

Cornmeal and Molasses Bread   *Makes 1 loaf*

This bread is delicious when toasted and spread with apple butter, or when used for sandwiches.

1 package Cornmeal and Molasses
Bread Mix

1 1/2 cups warm milk (105° to 115°F)

1/4 cup dark molasses

2 tablespoons unsalted butter,
melted

1. Oil a 9-inch loaf pan. Place the Cornmeal and Molasses Bread Mix in a large bowl. Make a well in the center and add the milk, molasses, and butter. Stir with a wooden spoon until the dough forms a ball.

2. Turn out onto a floured board and knead for 8 minutes. Place in an oiled bowl and cover with plastic wrap or a clean kitchen towel. Let rise until doubled in bulk, about 1 hour. Punch the dough down, shape into a loaf, and place in the prepared pan. Let rise until doubled in bulk again, about 45 minutes.

3. Preheat the oven to 375°F. Bake the bread for about 45 minutes, until golden brown and a toothpick inserted in the center comes out clean. Let cool in the pan on a wire rack. Remove from the pan and wrap in plastic. The bread will keep at room temperature for up to 4 days or in the freezer for up to 1 month.

Simply Sensational Beer Bread   *Makes 1 loaf*

1 package Simply Sensational Beer
Bread Mix

One 12-ounce can or bottle beer

1/2 cup (1 stick) unsalted butter,
melted

Preheat the oven to 400°F. In a large bowl, combine the Simply Sensational Beer Bread Mix, beer, and 1/4 cup of the butter, stirring well with a wooden spoon. Transfer the batter to a loaf pan and pour 2 tablespoons of the butter over the top. Bake for 50 to 60 minutes, until the loaf is golden brown and cooked through. Brush with the remaining 2 tablespoons butter and let cool for 20 minutes before removing from the pan. The bread will keep, wrapped in plastic wrap, at room temperature for up to 2 days or in the freezer for up to 1 month.

Bed and Breakfast Tray

This breakfast tray makes a lovely wedding or anniversary present, or you could give it to a friend who needs some cheering up. Arrange a pair of champagne flutes, a bottle of sparkling cider or champagne, the popover mixes, a small vase of flowers, and a book of poems on a white breakfast tray. Wrap the whole thing in clear cellophane and decorate with streamer ribbons in your favorite colors.

Cherry Pecan Popover Mix

Makes about 2 cups

1 cup all-purpose flour
1 teaspoon ground cinnamon
$1/2$ teaspoon ground ginger
2 tablespoons sugar
1 teaspoon salt
$1/2$ cup dried sweet cherries
$1/3$ cup chopped pecans

In a large bowl, combine the ingredients. Store in an airtight container and label with a 1-month expiration date.

Blueberry Walnut Popover Mix

Makes about $1^{1/2}$ cups

1 cup all-purpose flour
2 tablespoons sugar
1 teaspoon salt
$1/2$ cup unsweetened dried blueberries
$1/3$ cup chopped walnuts

In a large bowl, combine the ingredients. Store in an airtight container and label with a 1-month expiration date.

Cherry Pecan Popovers or Blueberry Walnut Popovers

Makes 6 popovers

1 package Cherry Pecan Popover Mix or Blueberry Walnut Popover Mix
1 cup milk

2 large eggs
2 tablespoon unsalted butter, melted

Preheat the oven to 425°F. Coat 6 popover cups, individual custard cups, or muffin cups with nonstick cooking spray and place in the oven to preheat for 5 minutes. In a medium-size bowl, whisk the Cherry Pecan Popover Mix or Blueberry Walnut Popover Mix with the milk, eggs, and butter. Divide the batter among the popover cups and bake for 15 minutes. Reduce the oven temperature to 350°F and continue to bake for 15 to 20 minutes, until puffed and browned. Serve immediately with butter and jam.

Weekend Breakfast Basket

If you are invited to the country for a weekend visit, this is a terrific gift to bring along. This basket has all the makings for a delicious breakfast. Line a picnic basket with attractive tea towels; include fresh oranges for juice, jam for the scones, a bag of coffee beans, a coffee grinder, and an assortment of herb teas; and decorate with ribbon streamers.

Maple Granola

Makes about 6 cups

$1/4$ cup sliced almonds
$1^1/3$ cups unsweetened flaked coconut
$3^1/2$ cups old-fashioned rolled oats
$1/3$ cup vegetable oil
1 cup maple syrup
$2/3$ cup golden raisins
$2/3$ cup chopped dates
$1/2$ cup chopped dried apples
$1/3$ cup chopped dried apricots

1. Preheat the oven to 350°F. Place the almonds and coconut in a jellyroll pan and place in the oven. Toast for about 10 minutes, until the coconut is golden brown. Transfer to a bowl to cool. Toast the oats in the same pan, stirring occasionally, for about 20 minutes, until lightly browned. Add to the bowl with the almonds and coconut.

2. In a small saucepan over medium heat, combine the oil and syrup and bring to a boil. Pour over the oat mixture and stir well to blend. Transfer to the jellyroll pan and bake for 15 minutes, until the mixture is crisp. Let cool, transfer to a large bowl, and add the remaining ingredients. Store the granola in an airtight container labeled with a 1-month expiration date and a note that it will keep in the freezer for up to 6 months.

Cranberry Oat Scone Mix

Makes about $3^1/2$ cups

$1^1/4$ cups old-fashioned rolled oats
1 cup all-purpose flour
$1/4$ cup sugar
1 teaspoon baking powder
1 cup unsweetened dried cranberries

In a small bowl, combine the ingredients. Store in an airtight container and label with a 3-month expiration date.

Cranberry Oat Scones   *Makes 8 to 10 scones*

Serve these scones warm, with butter, Devonshire cream, and jam.

One package Cranberry Oat Scone Mix

7 tablespoons cold unsalted butter, cut into ½-inch pieces

¼ cup heavy cream, plus more if needed

2 tablespoons milk

2 tablespoons sugar

1. Preheat the oven to 400°F. Line a baking sheet with a silicone baking mat, parchment paper, or aluminum foil. Place the Cranberry Oat Scone Mix in a large bowl. Cut in the butter with a fork or your fingers until the mixture resembles coarse meal. Sprinkle the heavy cream over the mixture and mix until the dough begins to form a ball. If the dough is dry, add more cream, 1 teaspoon at a time.

2. Transfer the dough to a floured board and roll out about ½ inch thick. Cut out 8 to 10 rounds with a 2-inch biscuit cutter. Reroll any scraps and cut out additional scones. Place on the prepared baking sheet, brush the tops with the milk, and sprinkle with the sugar. Bake for 12 to 15 minutes, until golden brown. Let cool for 3 minutes before serving warm. Or let cool completely and store in an airtight container at room temperature for up to 2 days or in the freezer for up to 1 month.

Lettuce Entertain You Basket

This unique gift would be perfect for a college grad just setting up his or her first apartment. It also is lovely for a wedding shower. Start with a large Lucite or wooden salad bowl and line it with a muslin lettuce storage bag. Add a coordinating pepper mill, several bottles of peppercorns, one bottle each of balsamic vinegar and extra-virgin olive oil, and packages of the delicious salad herb blends that follow. Wrap the bowl in a chef's apron, using the bib and apron strings to tie it neatly together. Slip salad servers through the "bow" as a decoration. Another idea would be to buy a salad spinner and fill it with the spice blends, muslin bag, pepper mill, vinegar, and oil. Just the blends, packed in small spice jars or tins, could be given in a muslin lettuce bag as a small hostess gift as well.

Tarragon Dressing Mix

Makes a little less than 1 cup

$1/2$ cup dried tarragon
$1/4$ cup dried thyme
2 tablespoons dry mustard
2 teaspoons salt
$1/2$ teaspoon garlic powder
1 teaspoon freshly ground black pepper

In a small bowl, combine the ingredients. Store in an airtight container and label with a 6-month expiration date.

Dilly Dressing Mix

Makes about 2 cups

$1/2$ cup dillweed
$1/2$ cup dried minced onion
$1/3$ cup dried parsley
$1/4$ cup dried basil
$1/4$ cup dried tarragon
2 tablespoons garlic salt
1 teaspoon celery salt
1 tablespoon freshly ground black pepper
1 teaspoon dried lemon peel

In a small bowl, combine the ingredients. Store in an airtight container and label with a 6-month expiration date.

Fiesta Herb Blend

Makes about 1 cup

A little taste of the Southwest, this warm and spicy herb blend is also terrific rubbed on chicken or fish before grilling.

$1/4$ cup chili powder
$1/4$ cup ground cumin
2 tablespoons garlic salt
2 tablespoons dried oregano
2 tablespoons dried minced onion

In a small bowl, combine the ingredients. Store in an airtight container and label with a 6-month expiration date.

Tarragon Dressing   *Makes about 1¹/₄ cups*

2 tablespoons fresh lemon juice

1 teaspoon Dijon mustard

1 tablespoon Tarragon Dressing Mix

1 cup olive oil

In a small bowl, whisk together the lemon juice and mustard. Blend in the Tarragon Dressing Mix and gradually add the oil, whisking until the mixture is smooth and creamy. The dressing will keep in the refrigerator for up to 1 week.

Fiesta Herb Dip   *Makes about 3¹/₄ cups*

Serve this dip with fresh vegetables and tortilla chips.

2 cups sour cream

¹/₂ cup mayonnaise

1 cup finely shredded mild cheddar cheese

3 tablespoons Fiesta Herb Blend

In a large bowl, stir together the sour cream, mayonnaise, cheese, and Fiesta Herb Blend. Cover with plastic wrap and refrigerate for at least 2 hours or up to 3 days.

Dilly Dressing   *Makes about 1¹/₄ cups*

Try this dressing on mixed greens or tossed into a pasta salad with seafood or chicken. It also makes a delicious topping for grilled seafood or baked potatoes.

³/₄ cup mayonnaise

¹/₂ cup milk

2 teaspoons Dilly Dressing Mix

In a small bowl, whisk together the mayonnaise and milk. Add the Dilly Dressing Mix and whisk until the mixture is smooth. Refrigerate for 2 hours before serving. The dressing will keep in the refrigerator for up to 1 week.

Fiesta Herb Dressing   *Makes about 2 cups*

1¹/₂ cups mayonnaise (lowfat is okay)

¹/₂ cup milk

2 tablespoons Fiesta Herb Blend

In a medium-size bowl, whisk the ingredients together until blended. Pour into a bottle and refrigerate for at least 2 hours or up to 3 days.

Dilly Dip   *Makes about 1¹/₂ cups*

1 cup sour cream or lowfat plain yogurt

¹/₂ cup mayonnaise (lowfat is okay)

2 tablespoons Dilly Dressing Mix

In a small bowl, whisk together the sour cream and mayonnaise. Fold in the Dilly Dressing Mix and whisk until the mixture is combined. Refrigerate for 2 hours before serving. The dip will keep in the refrigerator for up to 1 week.

Presto Pesto Basket

A bright red enamelware colander can hold four basics for a fabulous pasta dinner: a package of imported pasta, your homemade pestos, a package of breadsticks or a loaf of crusty bread, and a bottle of Italian red wine. Just add a checked table-cloth, napkins, and wineglasses, and you have a dynamite gift. Other ideas for this basket are to include fresh tomatoes and basil, good-quality extra-virgin olive oil, a chunk of your favorite Parmigiano-Reggiano cheese, and a small hand grater. Make sure to refrigerate the pesto until you are ready to pack it in the basket, and remind the recipient to refrigerate it when he or she unpacks the gift. Remember that pestos freeze beautifully, so if you are making them for your own use, freeze them in zipper-top plastic bags.

Sun-Dried Tomato Pesto

Makes about 3²/₃ cups

For each pound of pasta, toss one-quarter to one-third cup of pesto with the hot noodles. Garnish with additional Parmesan cheese and slivered fresh basil, if you like.

1 cup sun-dried tomatoes packed in oil
6 cloves garlic, peeled
¹/₂ cup olive oil
¹/₄ cup balsamic vinegar
¹/₂ cup packed fresh basil leaves
¹/₂ cup packed fresh Italian parsley leaves
1 cup freshly grated Parmesan cheese

Combine all the ingredients in a blender or food processor. Process for 15 seconds. Scrape down the bowl and process for 20 seconds. Transfer to a glass jar and refrigerate until ready to use. The pesto will keep in the refrigerator for up to 2 weeks.

Basil Pesto

Makes about 4 cups

Toss one-quarter to one-third cup of pesto with one pound freshly cooked pasta. Add cooked shrimp, scallops, or lobster for an over the top dinner.

2 cups packed fresh basil leaves
1 cup freshly grated Parmesan cheese
3 cloves garlic, peeled
¹/₄ cup pine nuts
¹/₂ cup olive oil, plus more for sealing
¹/₄ cup vegetable oil

In a blender or food processor, process the basil, Parmesan, garlic, and pine nuts. With the machine running, gradually add the oils and process until smooth. Pour into a glass jar, pour ¹/₂ inch olive oil on top to seal, cover, and refrigerate. The pesto will keep in the refrigerator for up to 1 week.

Flavored Vinegar Basket

Long before we decided that re-cycling was fashionable in America, Europeans were recycling wine bottles to store vinegar. This basket filled with homemade vinegars is simple to make, and the options for giving are endless. Whether you give a bottle of homemade vinegar with a recipe card attached; fill a basket with vinegars, croutons, good-quality olive oil, and a salad dressing bottle; or arrange every-thing in a salad bowl or salad spinner, flavored vinegars are nice additions to anyone's pantry.

Herb Vinegar

Makes about 1 quart

1 cup chopped fresh herbs, such as rosemary, chervil, thyme, basil, or oregano
4 or 5 whole black peppercorns
1 large clove garlic, halved
1 quart white wine vinegar or distilled white vinegar

Place the herbs in a 2-quart glass bowl. Add the peppercorns and garlic. Pour the vinegar over the herbs. Cover tightly with plastic wrap and let stand in a cool, dry place for 1 week. Strain the vinegar, pour into a glass bottle, and label with a 3-month expiration date.

Cinnamon Spice Vinegar

Makes 2 cups

2 cups distilled white vinegar
2 whole cinnamon sticks
1 tablespoon grated orange zest

Combine all the ingredients in a glass jar with an airtight seal. Let sit in a cool, dry place for 1 week. Strain the vinegar, pour into a glass bottle, and label with a 6-month expiration date.

Fruit-Flavored Vinegar

Makes about 1 quart

Fruit-flavored vinegars, once served only in five-star restaurants, are now available in the grocery store—for a high price. You can make this unusual and colorful gift by soaking the fruit overnight and then straining the liquid into a beautiful bottle that will show off its jewel-like color. I like to use rasp-berries, strawberries, blueberries, black-berries, peaches, nectarines, and plums when they are in season. If fresh fruit is not in season, use unsweetened frozen fruit; there is no need to defrost it first. I don't recommend leaving any fruit in the vinegar longer than overnight, as it will soon deteriorate and become unappealing.

2 cups chopped pitted fruit
1 quart distilled white vinegar

Place the fruit in a 2-quart glass bowl and pour the vinegar over the fruit. Cover tightly with plastic wrap and let stand at room temperature overnight. Strain the vinegar, pour into a glass bottle, and label with a 6-month expi-ration date.

House Vinaigrette   *Makes about ³/4 cup*

¼ cup Herb Vinegar
1 teaspoon Dijon mustard
1 teaspoon salt

1 clove garlic, crushed
⅔ cup extra-virgin olive oil

In a large glass bowl, whisk the Herb Vinegar and mustard together. Add the salt and garlic and whisk. Gradually add the oil and whisk until the mixture is smooth. Refrigerate for at least 3 hours before serving. The dressing will keep in the refrigerator for up to 4 days.

Fruity Vinaigrette   *Makes about 1¹/4 cups*

Serve this dressing over Bibb lettuce, mandarin oranges, sliced red onion, and slivered almonds.

¼ cup Fruit-Flavored Vinegar
¼ cup sugar
½ teaspoon salt

¼ cup chopped red onion
1 teaspoon Dijon mustard
⅔ cup canola oil

In a small bowl, whisk together the ingredients until blended. Use immediately or store in the refrigerator for up to 4 days.

Fruit Salad   *Serves 6*

1 cup canola oil
⅓ cup Cinnamon Spice Vinegar
2 tablespoons chopped fresh parsley
2 tablespoons honey

2 heads radicchio, cleaned and separated
1 Hass avocado, peeled and cut into 8 wedges
2 large navel oranges, peeled and cut into sections

In a small bowl, whisk together the oil, Cinnamon Spice Vinegar, parsley, and honey until blended. Place the radicchio on a plate and arrange the avocado wedges and orange sections in a fan shape over the radicchio. Drizzle with a few tablespoons of the dressing. Any leftover dressing will keep in the refrigerator for up to 4 days.

Soup's On Basket

"Mmm, mmm, good" is all I can say about these delicious mixes, which are combined with a few other ingredients to make a potful of comforting soup. This warm, homey basket can be given to a friend who's under the weather, or it can be a housewarming gift. If you would like to give this as a wedding shower or anniversary present, you can fill a soup pot with bags of the mixes and include a ladle tied to the top with two pretty tea towels to make a bow. Or store the soup mixes in jars and arrange the jars in a slow cooker or an attractive soup tureen. For a simple but terrific gift, pack a soup mix in a cellophane bag tied with raffia or ribbon and nest it in the bowl of a soup ladle or soup mug. My children gave these as gifts to their teachers one year, and they were a hit.

Spicy Lentil Soup Mix

Makes about 2 1/4 cups

A little cayenne spices up this comforting soup.

2 cups lentils
1/8 teaspoon cayenne pepper
1/2 teaspoon ground cumin
1 bay leaf
1 teaspoon garlic powder
4 teaspoons chicken bouillon granules, or 4 chicken bouillon cubes, crumbled

In a small bowl, combine the ingredients. Store in an airtight container and label with a 3-month expiration date.

Yellow Split Pea Soup Mix

Makes about 2 cups

2 cups yellow split peas
1 bay leaf
2 teaspoons chicken bouillon granules, or 2 chicken bouillon cubes, crumbled
2 teaspoons dried marjoram
1 teaspoon salt
1/2 teaspoon freshly ground black pepper

In a medium-size bowl, combine the ingredients and store in an airtight container. Or layer the ingredients in an attractive jar. Label with a 3-month expiration date.

Pasta e Fagioli Soup Mix

Makes about 2 1/4 cups

This simple but flavorful Italian soup mix can also be used as the basis for its own basket, packed with Focaccia Bread Mix (page 103) and the ingredients for putting together the soup. You could include a chunk of Parmigiano-Reggiano cheese, a cheese grater, and some Italian red wine, too.

1 cup dried small white beans
1/2 cup dried kidney beans
1/2 cup dried pink beans
4 teaspoons beef bouillon granules, or 4 beef bouillon cubes, crumbled
1 1/2 teaspoons dried rosemary
1 1/2 teaspoons salt
1/2 teaspoon freshly ground black pepper
1 1/2 cups elbow macaroni or your favorite small pasta

In a medium-size bowl, combine the beans, bouillon, rosemary, salt, and pepper. Store in an airtight container and label with a 3-month expiration date. Pack the macaroni in a separate airtight container.

Spicy Lentil Soup   *Serves 6*

2 tablespoons olive oil

1 cup chopped onion

1/2 cup chopped carrot

1/2 cup sliced celery

1/2 pound kielbasa or other smoked sausage, sliced into 1/2-inch-thick rounds

1 package Spicy Lentil Soup Mix

8 cups water

Heat the oil in a stockpot over medium heat. Add the onion, carrot, celery, and kielbasa and sauté until the vegetables soften and the sausage renders some of its fat. Remove any excess fat from the pan and add the Spicy Lentil Soup Mix. Stirring, cook the spices for 1 minute. Add the water and bring to a boil over high heat. Reduce the heat, cover, and simmer for about 1 1/2 hours, until the lentils are tender. Remove the bay leaf and serve immediately.

Yellow Split Pea Soup   *Serves 6*

2 tablespoons unsalted butter

1 cup chopped onion

1 1/2 cups sliced carrot

3/4 cup sliced celery

1 package Yellow Split Pea Soup Mix

8 cups water

Melt the butter in a stockpot over medium heat. Add the onion, carrot, and celery and cook until they begin to soften, about 5 minutes. Add the Yellow Split Pea Soup Mix, stirring to coat the peas. Add the water and bring to a boil over high heat. Reduce the heat, cover, and simmer for about 2 1/2 hours, until the peas are tender. Add more water during cooking if the soup becomes too thick. Remove the bay leaf and serve immediately.

Pasta e Fagioli Soup   *Serves 8*

1 pound sweet Italian sausage, casings removed

1 cup chopped onion

1 cup chopped carrot

1 cup chopped celery

One package Pasta e Fagioli Soup Mix

One 32-ounce can diced tomatoes, with their juice

8 cups water

Salt and freshly ground black pepper, if needed

In a large stockpot, sauté the sausage over medium heat, breaking it up into pieces, until no longer pink. Remove all but 1 tablespoon of the fat from the pan. Add the onion, carrot, and celery and sauté for about 4 minutes, until the vegetables soften. Add the Pasta e Fagioli Soup Mix (without the macaroni) and stir to blend. Add the tomatoes and bring to a boil over high heat, stirring up any browned bits from the bottom of the pan. Add the water, taste for seasoning, and add salt and/or pepper to taste, if needed. Lower the heat, cover, and simmer for about 2 hours, until the beans are tender. Taste for seasoning. Add the macaroni and simmer for 30 minutes. Serve immediately or refrigerate for up to 1 day before serving.

Luck of the Irish Basket

Your favorite Irishman or Irish-woman, or just about anyone else, will enjoy this gift on St. Patrick's Day. Line a white basket with green tissue, cellophane, or dish-towels, then add Irish coffee glasses, recipes for the Irish libations, a bottle of Jameson Irish Whiskey, a bag of coffee beans, and a shamrock plant for good luck. You can also include your favorite limericks, a book of Dylan Thomas's poetry, and a handwritten Irish toast, if you wish.

Irish Toasts

MAY THOSE WHO LOVE US LOVE US.
AND THOSE THAT DON'T LOVE US,
MAY GOD TURN THEIR HEARTS.
AND IF HE DOESN'T TURN THEIR HEARTS,
MAY HE TURN THEIR ANKLES,
SO WE'LL KNOW THEM BY THEIR LIMPING.

MAY YOUR GLASS BE EVER FULL.
MAY THE ROOF OVER YOUR HEAD BE
   ALWAYS STRONG.
AND MAY YOU BE IN HEAVEN HALF AN
   HOUR BEFORE THE DEVIL KNOWS
   YOU'RE DEAD.

HERE'S TO A FELLOW WHO SMILES
WHEN LIFE RUNS ALONG LIKE A SONG.
AND HERE'S TO THE LAD WHO CAN SMILE
WHEN EVERYTHING GOES DEAD WRONG.
MAY THE GOOD LORD TAKE A LIKING
   TO YOU,
. . . BUT NOT TOO SOON!

Irish Coffee   *Serves 1*

Smooth and strong, this is a great end to an evening.

1 tablespoon firmly packed dark
   brown sugar
3/4 cup hot coffee

1/4 cup Irish whiskey
1/4 cup whipped cream

Place the brown sugar in a mug or Irish coffee glass. Add the hot coffee and whiskey. Top with whipped cream and serve immediately.

Nutty Irishman Coffee   *Serves 1*

2 tablespoons Frangelico
2 tablespoons amaretto

3/4 cup hot coffee
1/4 cup whipped cream

Pour the Frangelico and amaretto into a mug or Irish coffee glass. Add the coffee. Top with whipped cream and serve immediately.

Lone Star Chili Basket

This stick-to-your-ribs chili and cornbread basket is a terrific gift for a weekend stay at a friend's home or for anyone in need of a little culinary inspiration. I like to pack a picnic or other wicker basket with white porcelain chili bowls, Black Bean Chili Mix, Southwestern Cornbread Mix, a ladle, tortilla chips, a six-pack of Lone Star beer (each bottle tied with a bandanna-print napkin), and six boot-shaped beer mugs. The chili mix is stored in two containers, one for the beans and another for the spice mixture; use a cellophane bag or jar for the beans and a small reusable jar for the spice blend.

Black Bean Chili Mix

Makes about ²/₃ cup

2 tablespoons dried oregano
¹/₄ cup finely ground yellow cornmeal
4 teaspoons chicken bouillon granules, or 4 chicken bouillon cubes, crumbled
2 tablespoons chili powder
1 tablespoon ground cumin
2 teaspoons salt
2 teaspoons sugar
2 cups dried black beans

In a medium-size bowl, combine all the ingredients except the black beans. Store in an airtight container and label with a 3-month expiration date. Store the black beans in an airtight container and label with a 4-month expiration date.

Southwestern Cornbread Mix

Makes about 2¹/₂ cups

Besides including it in this basket, you could give this mix in a basket with assorted breads. Either way, it's a nice gift for friends.

2 cups yellow cornmeal
2 cups all-purpose flour
1 tablespoon baking powder
1 teaspoon baking soda
¹/₃ cup sugar
¹/₈ to ¹/₄ teaspoon chipotle or other chili powder

In a large bowl, combine the ingredients. Store in an airtight container and label with a 3-month expiration date.

Black Bean Chili

Serves 8

1 package Black Bean Chili Mix

12 cups water

1/4 cup olive oil

1 pound chorizo or other spicy sausage, diced

1 cup seeded and chopped Anaheim chiles

1/2 cup chopped onion

1/2 cup chopped red bell pepper

1/2 cup chopped leek

3 cloves garlic, minced

2 cups fresh corn kernels or defrosted frozen corn

Salt and freshly ground black pepper

1. Place the black beans in a large bowl, add water to cover, and soak overnight. Drain and transfer to a large pot. Add 8 cups of the water and bring to a boil over high heat. Lower the heat and simmer, uncovered, for 2 hours. Drain and set aside.

2. In a 4-quart stockpot, heat the oil over medium heat. Add the sausage and sauté until it begins to render some fat, about 4 minutes. Remove all but 2 tablespoons of the fat from the pot. Add the chiles, onion, bell pepper, leek, and garlic and sauté for about 5 minutes, until the vegetables soften. Add the chili spice mix and sauté for 3 minutes, until the cornmeal is incorporated. Stir in the remaining 4 cups water and bring to a boil over high heat. Lower the heat and simmer, uncovered, for 30 minutes. Add the corn and black beans and simmer for 15 minutes, stirring occasionally. Season with salt and pepper to taste and serve immediately. The chili will keep in the refrigerator for up to 3 days or in the freezer for up to 2 months.

Southwestern Cornbread

Makes one 13 x 9-inch bread or 24 muffins

2 tablespoons unsalted butter

1/2 cup finely chopped onion

1/2 cup finely chopped red bell pepper

1 cup fresh corn kernels or defrosted frozen corn

1 package Southwestern Cornbread Mix

3 large eggs

2 cups milk

1/4 cup (1/2 stick) unsalted butter, melted

2 cups grated mild cheddar cheese

1. Preheat the oven to 400°F. Coat a 13 x 9-inch baking dish or 24 muffin cups with nonstick cooking spray. Melt the 2 tablespoons butter in a sauté pan over medium heat. Add the onion, bell pepper, and corn and sauté for 4 minutes, stirring. Let the mixture cool before continuing.

2. Place the Southwestern Cornbread Mix in a large bowl. Make a well in the center and add the eggs, milk, melted butter, cheese, and sautéed vegetables, stirring with a wooden spoon to blend. Transfer to the prepared pan and bake for 22 to 26 minutes (12 to 15 minutes for muffins), until a toothpick inserted in the center comes out clean. Remove from the oven and let cool for 15 minutes. Remove from the pan and serve. The cornbread will keep in an airtight container for up to 3 days.

Tea for Two Basket

This basket for tea lovers is the perfect birthday gift for a friend or holiday present for a favorite teacher or family member. If you have antiques stores in your area, you might be able to find an antique wire basket and teapot to start your basket, then fill it with teacups and saucers and these homemade tea mixes. Or give a white wicker tray laden with cups, saucers, a teapot, a tea strainer, and tea biscuits, either store-bought or homemade. Wrap these gifts in colored tissue paper, or leave them unwrapped and tie a wide grosgrain ribbon around everything. If a friend is under the weather, you can include a few magazines as well. For a simpler presentation, consider a vacuum-sealed canister or tea mug filled with spiced tea or a pretty teapot with a blended tea mix tied up in a cellophane bag.

Citrus Spiced Tea Mix

Makes about 3/4 cup

This tea mix will look and stay fresh when given in a sealed canister.

1/2 cup black tea leaves
12 whole cloves
1 teaspoon dried orange peel
1/2 teaspoon dried lemon peel
6 whole allspice berries
Three 1/2-inch cinnamon sticks, crushed

In a small bowl, combine the ingredients. Store in an airtight container and label with a 3-month expiration date.

Cranberry Apple Tea Mix

Makes about 1 1/2 cups

Ruby red with a hint of apple, this herbal tea is just the ticket for relaxing with a good book.

1 cup unsweetened dried cranberries
1/2 cup chamomile tea leaves
1/4 cup chopped dried apples

In a small bowl, combine the ingredients. Store in an airtight container and label with a 3-month expiration date.

Chai Tea Mix

Makes about 1 1/3 cups

Chai tea is simple to make using your own ingredients, and it's a welcome addition to a tea basket.

1 cup Darjeeling tea leaves
8 cardamom pods
6 whole cloves
Two 4-inch cinnamon sticks, crushed
1/2 teaspoon ground ginger
2 teaspoons whole allspice berries

In a small bowl, combine the ingredients. Store in an airtight container and label with a 3-month expiration date.

Citrus Spiced Tea   *Serves 2 to 4*

This tea is delicious served hot or cold.

1 tablespoon Citrus Spiced Tea Mix   Orange or lemon slices for garnish
4 cups boiling water

Place the Citrus Spiced Tea Mix in a teapot and add the boiling water. Let steep for 5 minutes, strain, and serve hot, garnished with orange slices. To serve cold, let the mixture steep, then strain and let cool to room temperature. Refrigerate and serve over ice.

Chai Tea   *Serves 2 to 4*

2 tablespoons Chai Tea Mix   Milk and sugar for serving
4 cups boiling water

Place the Chai Tea Mix in a teapot and add the boiling water. Let steep for 5 to 7 minutes, strain, and serve hot with milk and sugar.

Cranberry Apple Tea   *Serves 2 to 4*

1/4 cup Cranberry Apple Tea Mix   4 cups boiling water

Place the Cranberry Apple Tea Mix in a teapot and add the boiling water. Let steep for 5 to 7 minutes, then serve hot.

Great Grains Basket

This basket makes a great emergency kit for any cook. Everyone needs a quick side dish now and then, and these flavorful mixes fill the bill. Pack the mixes in clear canisters that can be reused, then arrange them in a wooden basket with kitchen towels and spatulas. Or buy a nice three-quart saucepan and nestle the mixes, wrapped in cellophane bags, into the pan. Wrap the pan in cellophane, tie up with ribbon, and insert a wooden spoon or spatula into the ribbon ties.

Brown Rice Pilaf Mix

Makes about $2^1/8$ cups

2 cups brown rice
3 teaspoons chicken bouillon granules, or 3 chicken bouillon cubes, crumbled
$1/2$ teaspoon freshly ground black pepper
$1/2$ teaspoon ground ginger
$1/4$ teaspoon ground cumin

In a medium-size bowl, combine the ingredients. Store in an airtight container and label with a 3-month expiration date.

Couscous Vegetable Salad Mix

Makes about 2 cups

1 cup quick-cooking couscous
1 teaspoon chicken bouillon granules, or 1 chicken bouillon cube, crumbled
1 cup dried currants
$1/2$ teaspoon dried cumin

In a small bowl, combine the ingredients. Store in an airtight container and label with a 3-month expiration date.

Cranberry Apricot Rice Mix

Makes about $2^2/3$ cups

4 teaspoons chicken bouillon granules, or 4 chicken bouillon cubes, crumbled
1 teaspoon dried lemon peel
1 teaspoon dried thyme
$1/3$ cup unsweetened dried cranberries
$1/3$ cup dried apricots, cut into small pieces
2 cups long-grain rice

In a medium-size bowl, combine the ingredients. Store in an airtight container and label with a 1-month expiration date.

Tabbouleh Mix

Makes about $1^1/4$ cups

1 cup bulgur (cracked wheat)
2 tablespoons dried parsley
2 tablespoons dried mint
1 teaspoon chicken bouillon granules, or 1 chicken bouillon cube, crumbled

In a small bowl, combine the ingredients. Store in an airtight container and label with a 3-month expiration date.

Sun-Dried Tomato Pilaf Mix

Makes about 2 1/2 cups

This colorful rice mix looks terrific when the ingredients are layered in a decorative glass jar.

2 cups long-grain rice
1/2 cup sun-dried tomatoes, not packed
   in oil
4 teaspoons chicken bouillon granules, or
   4 chicken bouillon cubes, crumbled
1 teaspoon garlic salt

In a medium-size bowl, combine the ingredients and store in an airtight container. Or layer the ingredients in an attractive jar. Label with a 4-month expiration date.

Brown Rice Pilaf   *Serves 6*

Try this hearty rice with chicken or seafood.

3 cups water
1 package Brown Rice Pilaf Mix
2 tablespoons soy sauce
1/3 cup dried currants

In a 2 1/2-quart saucepan, bring the water to a boil, then add the Brown Rice Pilaf Mix. Cover, reduce the heat, and simmer for 25 to 35 minutes, until the liquid is absorbed. Stir in the soy sauce and currants. Serve immediately.

Cranberry Apricot Rice   *Serves 6 to 8*

Studded with colorful fruit, this rice is a wonderful accompaniment to pork or poultry.

4 cups water
2 tablespoons unsalted butter or
   vegetable oil
1 package Cranberry Apricot Rice
   Mix

In a 2 1/2 quart saucepan, bring the water and butter to a boil. Add the Cranberry Apricot Rice Mix, cover, and reduce the heat. Simmer for about 20 minutes, until the rice is tender and the liquid is absorbed. Serve immediately.

Couscous Vegetable Salad   *Serves 4 to 6*

1 package Couscous Vegetable Salad Mix

$2/3$ cup boiling water

2 green onions, white and light green parts only, chopped

$1/2$ cup chopped red bell pepper

$1/2$ cup diced zucchini

$1/4$ cup olive oil

2 tablespoons fresh lemon juice

Place the Couscous Vegetable Salad Mix in a medium-size bowl and add the boiling water. Stir with a fork and let sit for about 5 minutes, until the water is absorbed. Stir in the green onions, bell pepper, zucchini, olive oil, and lemon juice. Serve at room temperature or chilled.

Sun-Dried Tomato Pilaf   *Serves 8*

Serve this pilaf with grilled seafood, meat, or poultry.

2 tablespoons unsalted butter

$1/2$ cup chopped onion

1 package Sun-Dried Tomato Pilaf Mix

4 cups water

$1/4$ to $1/2$ cup freshly grated Parmesan cheese, to your taste

In a $2^{1/2}$-quart saucepan, melt the butter over medium heat. Add the onion and sauté for about 4 minutes, until translucent. Add the Sun-Dried Tomato Pilaf Mix and stir until coated with butter. Add the water and bring to a boil. Cover, reduce the heat, and simmer for about 20 minutes, until the rice is tender and the liquid is absorbed. Stir in the Parmesan and serve immediately.

Tabbouleh   *Serves 6 to 8*

1 package Tabbouleh Mix

2 cups boiling water

$1/2$ cup minced onion

$1/2$ cup minced fresh parsley

$1/2$ cup minced fresh mint

1 cup seeded and chopped tomatoes

$1/2$ cup fresh lemon juice

$1/3$ cup olive oil

$1/2$ teaspoon freshly ground black pepper

Place the Tabbouleh Mix in a bowl and add the boiling water. Stir with a fork and let sit for 15 minutes. Drain through a sieve, then transfer to a bowl. Add the remaining ingredients and let stand for about 30 minutes. If not using immediately, refrigerate for up to 2 days. Serve at room temperature.

Bistro Basket

This bistro supper comes all wrapped up in a nice wicker basket lined with a tablecloth and napkins. Make sure to include two bottles of red wine—one for the stew and one to drink with dinner—as well as a corkscrew and wire whisk that can be tied through the ribbons that decorate the basket. Other versions of this over the top basket could include an oval Dutch oven filled with the mixes and wrapped in coordinating dishtowels secured with a ladle for the stew. For a simpler version, store the mixes in spice jars, tins, or cellophane bags and arrange them in a breadbasket.

Boeuf Bourguignon Mix

Makes about 1/3 cup

Nothing more than beef stew with a fancy name, boeuf bourguignon is simple to make, yet special enough to serve to guests.

5 teaspoons beef bouillon granules, or
    5 beef bouillon cubes, crumbled
1 bay leaf
2 teaspoons dried thyme
1 teaspoon salt
1/2 teaspoon freshly ground black
    pepper
3 tablespoons all-purpose flour

In a small bowl, combine the ingredients. Store in an airtight container and label with a 3-month expiration date.

Gallic Salad Seasoning Mix

Makes about 1/3 cup

You could store this seasoning mix in a cruet and give it, along with some good-quality olive oil and white wine vinegar, as a hostess gift.

1/4 cup dried tarragon
1 tablespoon dried thyme
2 teaspoons dried basil
2 teaspoons dillweed
1 teaspoon salt
1/4 teaspoon freshly ground black
    pepper

In a small bowl, combine the ingredients. Store in an airtight container and label with a 3-month expiration date.

French Bread Mix

Makes about 3 1/2 cups

A humble loaf of bread becomes majestic when served with boeuf bourguignon or with assorted cheeses and wine.

3 cups all-purpose flour
1/2 cup whole wheat flour
1 package active dry yeast
1 teaspoon salt
1 teaspoon sugar

In a large bowl, combine the ingredients. Store in an airtight container and label with a 3-month expiration date.

Boeuf Bourguignon   *Serves 6 to 8*

Serve this stew with steamed red potatoes and a green salad.

2 tablespoons olive oil

3 pounds boneless beef stew meat, cut into 1½-inch cubes

3 large onions, sliced

6 medium-size carrots, sliced into ½-inch-thick rounds

3 cloves garlic, crushed

1 package Boeuf Bourguignon Mix

One 14.5-ounce can chopped tomatoes, with their juice

1½ cups dry red wine

3 cups water

1. Preheat the oven to 325°F. Heat the oil in a 4-quart Dutch oven over high heat. Add the meat a few pieces at a time and brown, transferring the browned pieces to a platter. Add the onions, carrots, and garlic and sauté until the vegetables begin to soften. Add the Boeuf Bourguignon Mix and stir until the mix begins to melt into the vegetables. Add the tomatoes and bring to a boil. Return the meat to the pan and add the wine. Bring to a boil, stirring up any browned bits from the bottom of the pan.

2. Add the water, cover, and place in the oven for about 3 hours, until the meat is fork tender. Remove the meat and vegetables from the pan and set aside. Remove any fat from the cooking liquid and boil for about 10 minutes to reduce the liquid and concentrate the flavors. Remove the bay leaf, return the meat and vegetables to the pan, stir, and serve immediately.

French Bread   *Makes 2 loaves*

1 cup lukewarm water (105° to 115°F)

1 package French Bread Mix

1. Pour the water into a large bowl. Add the French Bread Mix and stir with a wooden spoon until blended and a dough forms. Turn the bread out onto a floured board and knead for 5 minutes, until smooth and elastic. Place in an oiled bowl and cover with plastic wrap. Let rise for 1 hour, until doubled in bulk. Punch the dough down and let rise for 1 hour more, until doubled in bulk again.

2. Oil a baking sheet. Form the dough into 2 loaves about 14 inches long and place on the prepared sheet. Let rise for about 40 minutes, until doubled in bulk. Preheat the oven to 400°F. Bake the bread for 20 minutes. Check the loaves to make sure they are not browning too quickly. If they are, cover loosely with aluminum foil. Continue baking for about 10 minutes more, until golden brown and crisp. Transfer to a wire rack and allow to cool. The bread will keep, wrapped in plastic, for up to 2 days.

Gallic Vinaigrette   *Makes about 1¼ cups*

1 cup olive oil

¼ cup white wine vinegar

2 tablespoons Dijon mustard

2 teaspoons Gallic Salad Seasoning Mix

In a small bowl, whisk together the oil, vinegar, mustard, and Gallic Salad Seasoning Mix. Refrigerate for at least 3 hours before serving with mixed greens or in a pasta salad. The dressing will keep in the refrigerator for up to 10 days.

Trattoria Basket

This simple basket includes an assortment of Italian ingredients to help your friends or family create wonderful meals with an Italian accent. I like to pack these items in a rustic basket or pasta bowl lined with a red tablecloth or dishtowels. Include bottles of good-quality extra-virgin olive oil and balsamic vinegar, a bulb of fresh garlic, a bottle of Italian wine, your home-made Italian Herb Mix and Focaccia Bread Mix, a chunk of Parmigiano-Reggiano cheese, a hand grater, and, if there's room, individual pasta bowls.

Italian Herb Mix

Makes about 1/2 cup

This versatile blend can be used to make a creamy dressing or an oil and vinegar–based dressing. The herbs can also be sprinkled over pizza or into pasta sauce, or blended with butter to spread on bread or grilled steak, chicken, or seafood.

1/4 cup dried basil
2 tablespoons dried oregano
1 tablespoon dried parsley
2 teaspoons garlic powder
1/2 teaspoon freshly ground black
  pepper
1 teaspoon sugar
1 teaspoon salt

In a small bowl, combine the ingredients. Store in an airtight container and label with a 6-month expiration date.

Focaccia Bread Mix

Makes about 6 1/8 cups

1/4 teaspoon sugar
2 teaspoons active dry yeast
6 cups all-purpose flour
1 teaspoon salt

In a large bowl, combine the ingredients. Store in an airtight container and label with a 3-month expiration date.

Creamy Italian Dressing   *Makes about 1 1/4 cups*

1 cup mayonnaise
2 tablespoons chopped red onion

2 tablespoons red wine vinegar
1 tablespoon Italian Herb Mix

In a small bowl, combine the mayonnaise, onion, vinegar, and Italian Herb Mix, whisking until smooth. Refrigerate for at least 1 hour before using. Serve over greens or as a dip for raw vegetables. The dressing will keep for up to 4 days in the refrigerator.

Italian Herb Dressing   *Makes about 1 1/3 cups*

1 cup olive oil
1/4 cup red wine vinegar

1 tablespoon Italian Herb Mix

In a small bowl, whisk together the oil, vinegar, and Italian Herb Mix until blended. Refrigerate for at least 2 hours before serving. The dressing will keep for up to 2 weeks in the refrigerator.

Seasoned Oil and Balsamic Vinegar Dipping Sauce   *Makes about 1 1/2 cups*

This delicious sauce is perfect as a dip for bread or vegetables, and it also makes a lovely sauce to serve over grilled chicken or seafood.

1 1/4 cups extra-virgin olive oil
1/4 cup balsamic vinegar
1 1/2 tablespoons Italian Herb Mix

In a small bowl, combine the oil, vinegar, and Italian Herb Mix, whisking until blended. Store at room temperature for up to 1 week or refrigerate for up to 1 month. Make sure to bring the sauce to room temperature before using, as the oil will solidify when refrigerated.

Quick Salsa di Pomodoro   *Makes about 4 cups*

A quick sauce to serve over your favorite pasta. Add canned Italian tuna or sweet or hot Italian sausage to the onion while sautéing, if you wish.

1/4 cup extra-virgin olive oil
1 1/2 cups chopped onion
1 tablespoon Italian Herb Mix
Two 32-ounce cans Italian plum tomatoes, crushed
Salt and freshly ground black pepper, if needed

In a 5-quart saucepan, heat the oil over medium heat. Add the onion and Italian Herb Mix and sauté for 3 to 4 minutes, until the onion is softened. Add the tomatoes and simmer, uncovered, for 30 minutes, stirring occasionally. Taste and add salt and/or pepper to taste, if needed. This sauce will keep in the freezer for up to 3 months.

Focaccia Bread   *Makes one 18 x 12-inch loaf*

1 package Focaccia Bread Mix
2 1/2 cups lukewarm water (105° to 115°F)
1/4 cup extra-virgin olive oil
1 1/2 tablespoons Italian Herb Mix

1. Place the Focaccia Bread Mix in a large bowl and add the water, 2 tablespoons of the oil, and 1 tablespoon of the Italian Herb Mix. Stir with a wooden spoon until the dough comes off the sides of the bowl and begins to form a ball. If you need to add more liquid, dribble in a tablespoon of water at a time. Turn the dough out onto a floured board and knead for about 5 minutes, until smooth and elastic. Transfer to an oiled bowl, cover with plastic wrap or a clean kitchen towel, and let rise in a draft-free place until doubled in bulk, 60 to 90 minutes.

2. Oil an 18 x 12-inch baking sheet. Punch the dough down and pat into the prepared sheet. Cover and let rise for 30 minutes. Preheat the oven to 425° F. Drizzle the remaining 2 tablespoons oil and 1/2 tablespoon Italian Herb Mix over the dough and bake for 25 to 30 minutes, until golden brown. Remove from the oven, cut with a pizza cutter, and serve warm. The focaccia will keep, wrapped in plastic, for up to 2 days.

Cinco de Mayo Basket

This portable Mexican fiesta is made up of a basket lined with a serape or colorful tablecloth and dried red chiles tied on the handles of the basket. Include a lidded acrylic pitcher, margarita glasses, coarse salt, gold tequila, and limes for the Margaritas Fantásticas, and avocados and a stoneware bowl for the Guacamole Olé. Make sure to include chips to go with the Salsa Fresca as well. Add a mariachi CD or your own mix of salsa favorites on a CD for the occasion.

Margaritas Fantásticas   *Serves 8*

2 limes, quartered

Coarse salt

1¼ cups fresh lime juice

1½ cups gold tequila

1¼ cups Triple Sec

2 cups ice cubes

2 limes, sliced, for garnish

Rub the rims of the margarita glasses with the lime quarters, then dip in coarse salt and place in the freezer. In a blender, combine the lime juice, tequila, Triple Sec, and ice cubes. Blend until the mixture is slushy. Pour into the prepared glasses and garnish with the lime slices.

Guacamole Olé   *Makes 3 cups*

4 Hass avocados

1 medium-size tomato, seeded and chopped

2 shallots, chopped

1 teaspoon fresh lime juice

1 clove garlic, crushed

2 tablespoons seeded and finely chopped Anaheim chile

1 teaspoon salt

Peel the avocados and mash them in a medium-size bowl with a fork. Add the remaining ingredients and stir to blend. Serve immediately, or spray the surface of the guacamole with nonstick cooking spray and cover with plastic wrap, pressing the wrap into the guacamole. Refrigerate for up to 1 day.

Salsa Fresca   *Makes about 4 cups*

1 jalapeño, seeded

½ cup chopped yellow onion

½ cup packed fresh cilantro sprigs

1 clove garlic

5 medium-size tomatoes, seeded and chopped

½ teaspoon ground cumin

1 teaspoon sugar

1½ tablespoons fresh lime juice

1½ teaspoons salt

¼ teaspoon freshly ground black pepper

Put the chile, onion, cilantro, and garlic in a food processor and process 3 or 4 times, until broken up. Add the tomatoes and pulse on and off about 5 times. Scrape down the sides, add the remaining ingredients, and puree or pulse to the desired consistency. (If you like a smoother sauce, puree; otherwise pulse.) Transfer to jars and label with a 2-week expiration date and a note to keep in the refrigerator.

Mardi Gras Basket

You don't have to travel to New Orleans to go a little Cajun. This gift showcases its festive flavors in an 8-quart stockpot for the recipient to use to create his or her own Fat Tuesday table. Begin the meal with Peppered Pecans, serve Seafood Gumbo as a perfect one-pot dinner (prepared in the stockpot), and finish off the meal with Chocolate Praline Sauce over vanilla ice cream. The Creole Shrimp Barbecue makes a nice appetizer or main dish in place of the gumbo. Decorate the stockpot with Mardi Gras coins, beads, and masks, and sprinkle purple, green, and gold confetti over the contents. Wrap the pot in bright tissue or cellophane, attaching noisemakers to the ribbons.

Peppered Pecans

Makes about 2 cups

2 tablespoons vegetable oil
$3/4$ cup sugar
1 tablespoon coarse salt
$1^1/2$ tablespoons freshly ground black pepper
$1/4$ teaspoon cayenne pepper
2 cups pecan halves

In a large skillet, heat the oil over low heat and add $1/2$ cup of the sugar, the salt, black pepper, and cayenne, stirring until combined. Add the pecans and toss to coat. Continue to toast, stirring constantly, for about 10 minutes, until the pecans are browned and fragrant. Remove from the heat and transfer to a bowl. Toss the hot nuts with the remaining $1/4$ cup sugar, making sure all the pecans are coated. Spread out on a baking sheet and let cool completely. Store in an airtight container. Label with a 6-month expiration date and a note to keep in the freezer.

Chocolate Praline Sauce

Makes about $1^3/4$ cups

This rich sauce is just the thing to serve over French vanilla ice cream. To be decadent, top brownies with scoops of ice cream and garnish with lots of sauce, whipped cream, and a cherry.

$1/2$ cup (1 stick) unsalted butter
$1/2$ cup pecan halves
$1/2$ cup firmly packed dark brown sugar
$3/4$ cup heavy cream
3 ounces bittersweet chocolate, finely chopped
1 teaspoon vanilla extract

In a heavy saucepan, melt the butter over medium-high heat. Add the pecans and toast for about 3 minutes, until fragrant. Lower the heat to medium, add the brown sugar, and cook until the mixture bubbles. Add the cream and simmer until the mixture begins to thicken, about 5 minutes. Add the chocolate, reduce the heat to low, and cook until the chocolate is melted and the sauce is smooth. Stir in the vanilla and remove from the heat. Serve warm. Or let cool to room temperature and transfer to a jar. Label with a 2-week expiration date and a note to keep in the refrigerator.

Gumbo Mix

Makes about ⁷/₈ cup

Gumbo is a simple one-pot dinner that can be prepared with your choice of seafood. To accompany it, include two cups of long-grain rice.

$^1/_2$ cup all-purpose flour
$1^1/_2$ teaspoons salt
$^1/_4$ teaspoon cayenne pepper
$^1/_8$ teaspoon freshly ground black
   pepper
1 teaspoon dried thyme
1 teaspoon dried oregano
1 bay leaf
5 teaspoons chicken bouillon granules,
   or 5 chicken bouillon cubes, crumbled

In a small bowl, combine the ingredients. Store in an airtight container and label with a 3-month expiration date.

Creole Seasoning Mix

Makes about $1^3/_4$ cups

1 cup salt
$^1/_4$ cup garlic powder
$^1/_4$ cup freshly ground black pepper
1 teaspoon cayenne pepper
$^1/_4$ cup sweet paprika
1 teaspoon dried oregano
1 teaspoon dried thyme

In a small bowl, combine the ingredients. Store in an airtight container and label with a 6-month expiration date.

Seafood Gumbo   *Serves 8*

Serve this over rice, garnished with chopped green onions.

$^1/_2$ cup vegetable oil
1 package Gumbo Mix
1 cup chopped yellow onion
1 cup chopped green bell pepper
1 cup chopped celery
6 cups water
2 pounds mixed shellfish (shrimp, crabmeat, scallops, clams, oysters, and/or crayfish), cleaned and shelled

1. In an 8-quart stockpot, heat the oil over medium-high heat and add the Gumbo Mix. Cook for about 3 minutes, stirring with a wire whisk, until dark amber. Add the onion, bell pepper, and celery and continue to cook, stirring, for 2 minutes. Lower the heat and cook for 2 minutes more, then add the water. Whisk the gumbo and bring to a boil over high heat. Lower the heat and simmer for 10 minutes. (If you plan to serve it later, remove it from the heat and refrigerate. When ready to serve, bring back to a boil over high heat.)

2. Bring the gumbo back to a boil over high heat and add the shellfish. Reduce the heat and simmer for 7 to 10 minutes, until the shellfish is just cooked through. (Shrimp should turn pink, scallops should be opaque, and the shells of clams or oysters should be open.) Remove from the heat and skim any fat from the top. Remove the bay leaf and serve.

Creole Shrimp Barbecue   *Serves 4*

Spicy and buttery, these shrimp are delicious served over rice as an entrée or alone as an appetizer. Crusty bread will help soak up the sauce.

24 large shrimp, shelled and deveined
$^3/_4$ cup ($1^1/_2$ sticks) cold unsalted butter, cut into 1-inch pieces
$1^1/_2$ teaspoons Creole Seasoning Mix
$^1/_4$ cup Worcestershire sauce
2 cloves garlic, chopped
$^1/_4$ cup fresh lemon juice

Preheat the oven to 450°F. Place the shrimp in an ovenproof sauté pan. Dot with half of the butter, then sprinkle with the Creole Seasoning Mix, Worcestershire sauce, and garlic. Bake for 3 to 4 minutes. Turn the shrimp and bake for another 2 minutes. Transfer the pan to the stovetop and place over medium-high heat. Add the lemon juice and whisk in the remaining butter. Serve immediately.

Chocoholic's Basket

Chocolate lovers are a breed unto themselves: they can sniff chocolate anywhere, and they eat chocolate in every possible variation. This basket is a chocolate lover's delight, with two types of hot chocolate and some amazing chocolate chunk cookies. Pack this gift in a basket and include mugs, along with a microplane grater for grating chocolate over the tops of the drinks, a bar of good-quality chocolate, a package of freshly baked Triple Chocolate Cookies, and chocolate spoons, which you can buy at gourmet retailers or make yourself.

Chocolate Spoons

Makes 6 spoons

These are simple to make and elegant to give. If you would like to flavor the chocolate, stir two teaspoons of your favorite liqueur into the melted chocolate.

1½ cups chopped semisweet chocolate
6 plastic spoons

Place the chocolate in a microwavable bowl and microwave on high for 1 minute. Stir the chocolate and microwave for 20 to 30 seconds, until it is melted. Dip the bowl of a spoon into the chocolate and allow any excess to drip off into the bowl. Place the spoon on waxed paper to dry. Repeat until all the spoons are coated. Store the spoons in an airtight container or wrap individually in cellophane bags and tie with ribbons. They will keep for up to 1 month at room temperature.

White Hot Chocolate Mix

Makes about 1 cup

1 cup grated white chocolate
1½ teaspoons dried orange peel
2 teaspoons vanilla powder

In a small bowl, combine the ingredients. Store in an airtight container and label with a 3-month expiration date.

Mexican Wicked Hot Chocolate Mix

Makes about 3¼ cups

This spicy chocolate mix combines cinnamon and a kick of cayenne to warm up any cold winter day.

½ cup firmly packed light brown sugar
¾ teaspoon ground cinnamon
2 teaspoons vanilla powder
⅓ cup cocoa powder
2½ cups powdered milk
⅛ teaspoon cayenne pepper

In a medium-size bowl, combine the ingredients. Store in an airtight container and label with a 3-month expiration date.

Triple Chocolate Cookies

Makes about 3 dozen cookies

These cookies are awesome for ice cream sandwiches: use coffee, mint chip, vanilla, or strawberry ice cream, then roll the edge in your favorite nuts or sprinkles.

3/4 cup (1 1/2 sticks) unsalted butter
2/3 cup granulated sugar
1/3 cup firmly packed light brown sugar
1 large egg
1 teaspoon vanilla extract
1 1/2 cups all-purpose flour
1/3 cup Dutch process cocoa
3/4 cup dark chocolate cut into 1/2-inch pieces
1/2 cup white chocolate cut into 1/2-inch pieces

1. Preheat the oven to 325°F. Line 2 baking sheets with silicone baking mats, parchment paper, or aluminum foil. In a large bowl using an electric mixer, cream together the butter and sugars until smooth. Add the egg and vanilla and continue beating. Add the flour, cocoa, and chocolate pieces, beating at low speed until just blended.

2. Roll the dough into golf ball–size rounds and place 2 inches apart on the prepared baking sheets. Wet your hands and press the cookies down so they are 1/2 inch thick. Bake for 12 to 15 minutes, until the tops look dry. Let cool on the baking sheets for 5 minutes, then transfer to a wire rack to cool completely. The cookies will keep in an airtight container at room temperature for up to 4 days or in the freezer for up to 2 months.

White Hot Chocolate

Serves 4

4 cups milk
1/2 cup heavy cream
1/2 cup White Hot Chocolate Mix

Grated bittersweet chocolate for garnish

In a small saucepan, heat the milk and cream over medium heat until bubbles form around the edge. Add the White Hot Chocolate Mix and whisk until the chocolate is melted. Continue to whisk until the mixture is hot. Serve in heated mugs or stir into strong hot coffee. Garnish with grated bittersweet chocolate.

Mexican Wicked Hot Chocolate

Serves 6

3 cups water
One package Mexican Wicked Hot
  Chocolate Mix

Whipped cream for garnish

Heat the water to boiling and add the Mexican Hot Chocolate Mix. Stir with a whisk until smooth. Simmer for 2 minutes. Divide the hot chocolate among 6 mugs and garnish with whipped cream. For a frothier hot chocolate, remove from the heat and use an immersion blender to blend the chocolate.

Hot Chocolate

Let Them Eat Cake Basket

Marie Antoinette had the right idea when she uttered that famous line, and your friends will love you for giving them this selection of blue-ribbon cake mixes. Use a 13 x 9-inch baking pan, bundt pan, large flour sifter, or covered cake plate as your gift basket and fill it with packages of your prepared cake mixes, with recipe tags tied to each. Wrap your gifts in dishtowels or cellophane, tie up with ribbon, and then insert crossed spatulas or wooden spoons through the ribbon to decorate your basket.

Carrot Cake Mix

Makes about 5 2/3 cups

2 cups sugar
2 teaspoons vanilla powder
1/2 cup chopped pecans (optional)
3 cups all-purpose flour
2 teaspoons baking soda
2 teaspoons ground cinnamon
1/8 teaspoon ground nutmeg

In a large bowl, combine the ingredients and store in an airtight container. Or layer the ingredients in an attractive jar. Label with a 1-month expiration date. If you omit the pecans, label with a 3-month expiration date.

Spiced Apple Cake Mix

Makes about 6 cups

You may omit the raisins and walnuts and label the mix with a three-month expiration date. If you do, be sure to include the nuts and raisins in the recipe instructions.

3 cups all-purpose flour
1 1/2 cups sugar
1 1/2 teaspoons baking soda
1 teaspoon vanilla powder
1 1/2 teaspoons ground cinnamon

1/4 teaspoon ground nutmeg
1 cup chopped walnuts
1/2 cup golden raisins

In a large bowl, combine the ingredients and store in an airtight container. Or layer the ingredients in an attractive jar. Label with a 1-month expiration date.

Chocolate Brownie Cake Mix

Makes about 7 1/2 cups

You may omit the nuts and label with a three-month expiration date. If you do, be sure to include the nuts in the recipe instructions.

2 1/2 cups all-purpose flour
2 1/2 cups sugar
2/3 cup Dutch process cocoa
2 tablespoons instant coffee granules
2 teaspoons baking soda
1 1/2 cups chopped walnuts
2 teaspoons vanilla powder

In a large bowl, combine the ingredients and store in an airtight container. Or layer the ingredients in an attractive jar. Label with a 1-month expiration date.

Carrot Cake   *Makes one 13 x 9-inch sheet cake*

This is great with vanilla ice cream.

1 package Carrot Cake Mix

1½ cups canola oil

3 large eggs

3 cups grated carrot

One 8-ounce can crushed pineapple, with its juice

Confectioners' sugar for dusting

Preheat the oven to 350°F. Coat the inside of a 13 x 9-inch baking pan with nonstick cooking spray. Place the Carrot Cake Mix in a large bowl and make a well in the center. Add the oil, eggs, carrot, and pineapple. Blend until combined. Pour into the prepared baking pan and bake for 40 to 50 minutes, until a cake tester inserted in the center comes out clean. Let cool in the pan, then dust with confectioners' sugar. The cake will keep, tightly covered, in the refrigerator for up to 5 days.

Spiced Apple Cake   *Makes 1 bundt cake*

This tall cake is terrific for breakfast, as well as for dessert. Serve it warm with fresh fruit or vanilla ice cream.

1 package Spiced Apple Cake Mix

1½ cups canola oil

3 large eggs

3 cups chopped apples (Golden Delicious, Granny Smith, and/or Gala)

Preheat the oven to 350°F. Coat a bundt or tube pan with nonstick cooking spray. Place the Spiced Apple Cake Mix in a large bowl and make a well in the center. Add the oil, eggs, and apples and stir until the mixture is well combined. Pour into the prepared pan and bake for about 70 minutes, until a toothpick inserted in the center comes out clean. Let cool and remove from the pan. The cake will keep in an airtight container in the refrigerator for up to 5 days.

Chocolate Brownie Cake   *Makes 1 bundt cake*

Rich and dense, this chocolate cake is awesome served with a scoop of vanilla ice cream and hot fudge sauce.

3 cups sour cream (lowfat is okay)

2 large eggs

½ cup canola oil

1 package Chocolate Brownie Cake Mix

Preheat the oven to 350°F. Coat a tube or bundt pan with nonstick cooking spray. In a large bowl using an electric mixer, beat together the sour cream, eggs, and oil until combined. Add the Chocolate Brownie Cake Mix and beat on low until the ingredients are blended. Pour the batter into the prepared pan and bake for about 70 minutes, until a cake tester inserted in the center comes out clean. Allow the cake to cool in the pan for 15 to 20 minutes, then remove it from the pan and let cool on a wire rack. When the cake is completely cooled, wrap in plastic and refrigerate for easier slicing. The cake will keep in the refrigerator for up to 5 days.

Sundae Best Basket

This instant party basket is just the ticket to liven up a weeknight with friends or to take to a family reunion. A large basket or large serving tray can hold sundae glasses, an ice cream scoop, long-handled spoons, jars of homemade sauces, and assorted prepackaged toppings, such as nuts, candies, and a jar of maraschino cherries. To go over the top, include an ice cream maker.

World's Best Hot Fudge Sauce

Makes about 2 cups

Smooth, rich, glossy, and not too sweet, this is by far the world's best hot fudge sauce.

1/2 cup (1 stick) unsalted butter
4 ounces unsweetened chocolate
1 1/2 cups sugar
1 cup evaporated milk

In a small saucepan, melt the butter and chocolate over medium heat. Stir in the sugar and evaporated milk, whisking until smooth. Transfer to an airtight container and let cool completely. The sauce will keep in the refrigerator for 2 weeks and should be reheated before serving.

Raspberry Sauce

Makes about 3 1/2 cups

This sophisticated sauce is deceptively easy to make and delicious to boot. It's great with vanilla ice cream or pound cake.

4 cups fresh or defrosted frozen raspberries
1 cup sugar, plus more if needed
2 teaspoons fresh lemon juice

Combine the ingredients in a small saucepan and bring to a boil over high heat. Lower the heat and simmer for 3 minutes, stirring constantly. Taste the sauce and correct for sweetness, adding more sugar if necessary. Strain through a fine-mesh sieve into an airtight container and let cool completely. The sauce will keep in the refrigerator for up to 2 weeks.

Milk Chocolate Peanut Butter Sauce

Makes about 1 3/4 cups

A bit like a Reese's Peanut Butter Cup, this sauce is awesome over ice cream or slices of cake.

1 tablespoon unsalted butter
2 tablespoons firmly packed light brown sugar
1 tablespoon light corn syrup
1/4 cup chunky peanut butter
1/2 cup heavy cream
3/4 cup chopped milk chocolate

In a small heavy saucepan, combine the butter, brown sugar, and corn syrup over medium heat. When the butter is melted, whisk in the peanut butter and cream and bring to a boil. Remove from the heat and add the chocolate, whisking until the chocolate is melted. Transfer to an airtight container and let cool completely. The sauce will keep in the refrigerator for 2 weeks and should be reheated before serving.

Pralines and Cream Sauce

Makes about 4 1/4 cups

Straight from New Orleans, this smooth sauce studded with pecans is perfect over ice cream.

6 tablespoons (3/4 stick) unsalted butter
1 1/2 cups pecan halves
1 1/2 cups granulated sugar
3/4 cup firmly packed light brown sugar
1/2 cup heavy cream
1 tablespoon bourbon

In a small saucepan, melt the butter over medium heat. Add the pecans and toast for about 1 minute, until lightly browned. Add the sugars and stir until they begin to melt. Add the cream and bring to a boil, stirring until the mixture is blended. Remove from the heat and stir in the bourbon. Transfer to an airtight container and let cool completely. The sauce will keep in the refrigerator for 2 weeks and should be reheated before serving.

Wok on the Wild Side Basket

*Here ingredients needed to make a
stir-fried noodle dish are nestled
into a wok along with a stir-fry
spatula, cleaver, ginger grater or
microplane grater, six rice bowls,
and six sets of chopsticks with rests.
Include a steamer, Asian noodles, a
knob of fresh ginger, toasted sesame
oil, sesame seeds, soy sauce, rice
wine vinegar, cornstarch, and for-
tune cookies, which can be found
in most supermarkets. Include the
recipe for this simple stir-fry, too.
Wrap the wok in cellophane, decorate it with your favorite colored
ribbons, and cross long cooking
chopsticks through the ribbons.*

Stir-Fry with Noodles   *Serves 6*

1/2 pound chicken, fish, or beef, cut
  into 1/2-inch strips

2 teaspoons rice wine vinegar

2 tablespoons soy sauce

1 teaspoon cornstarch

1/4 cup canola oil

1 teaspoon peeled and grated
  fresh ginger

1 clove garlic, chopped

1 cup chopped napa cabbage

1/2 cup chopped green onions,
  white and light green parts

1/2 cup coarsely grated carrot

One 8-ounce package Chinese
  noodles, cooked *al dente*

3 tablespoons soy sauce

1 tablespoon toasted sesame oil

1 tablespoon toasted sesame
  seeds

1. In a medium-size bowl, combine the chicken, vinegar, soy
sauce, and cornstarch. Marinate in the refrigerator for 30 minutes. In a wok, heat 2 tablespoons of the canola oil over high
heat, add the chicken mixture, and stir-fry for about 1 minute,
until the meat is white or light brown. Transfer to a plate and
cover.

2. Heat the remaining 2 tablespoons canola oil in the wok
and add the ginger and garlic. Stir-fry, stirring constantly, for
30 seconds, then add the cabbage, green onions, and carrot.
Continue to stir-fry until crisp but tender, about 3 minutes.
Add the noodles and soy sauce and return the chicken to the
wok. Stir-fry for 3 minutes. Add the sesame oil and sesame seeds
and mix well. Serve immediately.

Make Lemonade Basket

Sunny lemons are a refreshing basket filler, but you can also include homemade Limoncello, an Italian liqueur that you can make for a fraction of the cost of a bottle in your local liquor store, and a dynamite Lemon Pound Cake Mix to bake and then soak in a syrup and cover with a glaze made from the lemons in the basket. Top that all off with an acrylic pitcher to serve lemonade, and you have a sunny basket to brighten anyone's day.

Lemon Pound Cake Mix

Makes about 5 1/4 cups

This moist, melt-in-your-mouth cake is a favorite for picnics and barbecues.

2 cups sugar
3 cups all-purpose flour
1/2 teaspoon baking powder
1/2 teaspoon baking soda
1 teaspoon salt
3 tablespoons powdered buttermilk

In a large bowl, combine the ingredients. Store in an airtight container and label with a 3-month expiration date.

Limoncello

Makes about 6 cups

This zesty liqueur is a digestive aid. Most Italian households have their own homemade versions, which often come out at the end of a meal. This is my cousin Nella's recipe.

3 cups vodka
Grated zest of 6 lemons
1 3/4 cups sugar
2 cups water

Place the vodka and zest in a jar and allow to soak for 3 to 4 days. Strain out the zest and discard. In a 3-quart saucepan over high heat, combine the sugar and water and bring to a boil. Let boil for 3 minutes, then remove from the heat and let cool. Add to the vodka and refrigerate for 1 week before serving. Pour into a bottle and label with a 6-month expiration date and a note to keep in the refrigerator.

Lemon Pound Cake   *Makes 1 bundt cake*

Try serving this with fresh strawberries or a cup of hot tea.

1 cup (2 sticks) unsalted butter, softened

4 large eggs

1 teaspoon lemon oil or grated zest of 3 lemons

1/4 cup fresh lemon juice

3/4 cup water

1 package Lemon Pound Cake Mix

1 recipe Lemon Syrup

1 recipe Lemon Glaze

1. Preheat the oven to 350°F. Coat a bundt or tube pan with nonstick cooking spray. In a large bowl using an electric mixer, beat together the butter, eggs, lemon oil, lemon juice, and water. Add the Lemon Pound Cake Mix and beat until the mixture is smooth. Pour into the prepared pan and bake for about 70 minutes, until a cake tester inserted in the center comes out clean. Let cool in the pan on a wire rack for 15 minutes.

2. Meanwhile, make the Lemon Syrup and Lemon Glaze. Poke a few holes in the top of the cake and spoon the syrup over the cake. When it has cooled completely, transfer to a wire rack and pour the glaze over the cake, letting it drizzle down the sides. The cake will keep in an airtight container in the refrigerator for up to 5 days.

Lemon Syrup   *Makes about 1 cup*

1/2 cup sugar

1/2 cup fresh lemon juice

Combine the sugar and lemon juice in a medium-size saucepan and cook over low heat until the sugar dissolves.

Lemon Glaze   *Makes about 2 1/4 cups*

2 cups sifted confectioners' sugar   1/4 cup fresh lemon juice

In a large bowl, whisk together the confectioners' sugar and lemon juice until the sugar dissolves.

Fresh Lemonade   *Serves 10*

4 cups cold water

2 1/2 cups superfine sugar

2 1/2 cups fresh lemon juice, strained (about 15 lemons)

Thinly sliced lemons for garnish

In a 2-quart pitcher, stir together the water and superfine sugar until the sugar dissolves. Add the lemon juice and stir until blended. Taste for sweet-tartness, adding more sugar, water, or lemon juice to suit your taste. Refrigerate for at least 2 hours before serving. Garnish each glass with a lemon slice.

Grillin' and Chillin' Basket

Perfect for Father's Day or for a friend with a new grill, these rubs can be packed into a basket or arranged on a steak platter or in a grill basket. Add skewers, a meat fork with an integrated thermometer, a set of steak knives, assorted wood chips for smoking, oven mitts, and barbecue tools. For Dad, make sure to get a fun apron for him to wear while grilling and use it to wrap your gift.

Seafood Rub Mix

Makes about $1/4$ cup

This unique blend brings out the flavor in grilled seafood.

$1/2$ teaspoon salt
1 teaspoon garlic powder
1 tablespoon sweet paprika
1 teaspoon dried oregano
$1/8$ teaspoon ground nutmeg
$1/4$ teaspoon freshly ground black
   pepper
$1/4$ teaspoon dried lemon peel

In a small bowl, combine the ingredients. Store in an airtight container and label with a 6-month expiration date.

Cajun Barbecued Beef Rub Mix

Makes a generous $3/4$ cup

This mix gives steaks and roasts a sweet and spicy kick. It's great on burgers, too.

2 tablespoons freshly ground black
   pepper
2 tablespoons garlic powder
2 tablespoons salt
2 tablespoons firmly packed light brown
   sugar
2 tablespoons dried oregano
1 tablespoon fennel seeds
1 tablespoon dry mustard
$11/2$ teaspoons sweet paprika
1 teaspoon cayenne pepper

In a small bowl, combine the ingredients. Store in an airtight container and label with a 6-month expiration date.

Grilled Fish Fillets   *Serves 6*

Swordfish, sea bass, and salmon work well here.

6 fish fillets, cut about 1 inch thick
   (about $1/3$ pound each)
$1/3$ cup olive oil
2 tablespoons fresh lemon or lime
   juice, plus more for serving
2 teaspoons Seafood Rub Mix

Place the fish fillets in a flat dish. Combine the oil, lemon juice, and Seafood Rub Mix in a small bowl and paint the mixture on the fillets. Cover with plastic wrap and refrigerate for at least 20 minute or up to 2 hours. Meanwhile, preheat a charcoal grill until the coals are white, or preheat a gas grill for 10 minutes. Grill the fish for 3 to 4 minutes per side, until firm and cooked through. Remove from the grill and serve with additional lemon juice.

Cajun Barbecued Beef   *Serves 6*

$1/3$ cup olive oil
2 tablespoons Cajun Barbecued
   Beef Rub Mix
6 rib-eye steaks, cut about $3/4$ inch
   thick

Combine the oil and Cajun Barbecued Beef Rub Mix in a large glass dish. Add the steaks and turn to coat. Marinate in the refrigerator for 1 hour. Meanwhile, preheat a charcoal grill until the coals are white, or preheat a gas grill for 10 minutes. Grill the steaks to the desired doneness and serve.

Coffee Aficionado's Basket

Coffee lovers, like chocoholics, just can't seem to get enough of a good thing, and this basket filled with coffee beans (decaf and regular), a coffee grinder, flavored syrups, coffee mugs, and two dynamite coffee cake mixes is sure to please your favorite coffee aficionado. Whether you give this as a hostess gift, wedding shower present, a birthday present, or housewarming gift, it's a winner. A basket is the perfect container, although you could use a plain box and line it with different-colored tissue paper, cellophane, or straw. Cover the box with coffee-themed wrapping paper—either something with coffee cups or mugs or just brown-toned paper. If you are really crafty, you can cover the box with burlap, like a sack of coffee beans.

Nutty Streusel Topping Mix

Makes a little over 3 cups

$3/4$ cup all-purpose flour
$1 1/4$ cups firmly packed light brown
  sugar
1 tablespoon ground cinnamon
1 cup chopped pecans, walnuts, or
  almonds

In a medium-size bowl, combine the ingredients. Store in an airtight container and label with a 1-month expiration date.

Coffee Cake Mix

Makes a little over $3 1/2$ cups

$2 1/4$ cups all-purpose flour
$1 1/4$ cups sugar
2 teaspoons baking powder
$1/2$ teaspoon baking soda
$1/2$ teaspoon salt
1 tablespoon vanilla powder

In a medium-size bowl, combine the ingredients. Store in an airtight container and label with a 3-month expiration date.

Basic Streusel Topping Mix

Makes about $3/4$ cup

$1/3$ cup all-purpose flour
$1/2$ cup firmly packed light brown sugar
$1/2$ teaspoon ground cinnamon

In a small bowl, combine the ingredients. Store in an airtight container and label with a 3-month expiration date.

Banana Chocolate Chip Bread Mix

Makes about $3 1/4$ cups

1 cup All-Bran cereal
$1 1/3$ cups all-purpose flour
$1/3$ cup sugar
$1/2$ cup semisweet chocolate chips
$1 1/2$ teaspoons baking powder
1 teaspoon vanilla powder

In a medium-size bowl, combine the ingredients. Store in an airtight container and label with a 3-month expiration date.

Nutty Streusel Topping

Makes enough for 1 coffee cake

1 package Nutty Streusel Topping Mix

3 tablespoons cold unsalted butter

Empty the Nutty Streusel Topping Mix into a large bowl. Cut in the butter until the mixture is crumbly.

Basic Streusel Topping

Makes enough for 1 bread

1/4 cup (1/2 stick) unsalted butter, cut into 1/2-inch pieces

1 package Basic Streusel Topping Mix

In a small bowl, cut the butter into the Basic Streusel Topping Mix until it resembles small peas.

Coffee Cake

Makes 1 bundt cake

One package Coffee Cake Mix

3/4 cup (1 1/2 sticks) unsalted butter, cut into small pieces

4 large eggs

1 1/2 cups sour cream

1 recipe Nutty Streusel Topping

1. Preheat the oven to 350°F. Coat a 10-cup bundt or tube pan with nonstick cooking spray. In a large bowl using an electric mixer, beat the Coffee Cake Mix and butter on low speed until crumbly. Add the eggs, one at a time, and then the sour cream. Beat until the mixture is smooth.

2. Transfer half of the batter to the prepared pan and top with half of the Nutty Streusel Topping. Add the remaining batter and sprinkle with the rest of the topping. Bake for 45 to 55 minutes, until a cake tester inserted in the center comes out clean. Let cool for 30 minutes before removing from the pan. The cake will keep in an airtight container for up to 4 days.

Banana Chocolate Chip Bread

Makes one 8-inch square or round bread

One package Banana Chocolate Chip Bread Mix

1/2 cup milk

2 medium-size ripe bananas, mashed

1 large egg

1/4 cup canola oil

1 recipe Basic Streusel Topping

Preheat the oven to 400°F. Coat an 8-inch square or round pan with nonstick cooking spray. Place the mix in a large bowl. One at a time, add the milk, bananas, egg, and oil, stirring until the batter is blended. Pour into the prepared pan and top with the Basic Streusel Topping. Bake for 20 to 25 minutes, until a toothpick inserted in the center comes out clean. Let cool in the pan on a wire rack for 20 minutes before serving. The cake will keep, tightly covered, in the refrigerator for up to 5 days.

Hooray for the Red, White, and Blue Basket

How fortunate that just when we celebrate Independence Day, red and blue berries are growing in abundance. Take advantage of that coincidence and build your gift to a holiday host around them. Place filled berry baskets in a larger basket lined with red-and-white-checked dishtowels or napkins. Add homemade mixes packed in cellophane bags or jars and decorated with tricolor ribbons or fabric to attach the recipe tags. You could also present the Cobbler Mix and some berries in a 13 x 9-inch baking dish, the Blueberry Popover Pancake Mix in a 9-inch pie plate, or the Strawberry Shortcake Mix in a large mixing bowl. Wrap them in coordinating dishtowels or cellophane, then decorate with red, white, and blue ribbons.

Cobbler Mix

Makes about 2 cups

1 cup all-purpose flour
1 cup sugar
1 teaspoon baking powder
1 teaspoon vanilla powder

In a medium-size bowl, combine the ingredients. Store in an airtight container and label with a 3-month expiration date.

Blueberry Popover Pancake Mix

Makes about 1 1/3 cups

I love popovers, pancakes, and blueberries, so when I came up with this mix, I was in heaven. The mix makes a pancake that tastes like a popover but is baked in a nine-inch pie plate. It sends out luscious aromas while baking. What a wake-up call on a summer Saturday morning!

1 teaspoon vanilla powder
1/4 teaspoon salt
1/4 teaspoon ground nutmeg
1/4 cup sugar
1 cup all-purpose flour

In a small bowl, combine the ingredients. Store in an airtight container and label with a 3-month expiration date.

Strawberry Shortcake Mix

Makes about 2 1/2 cups

My family's favorite Fourth of July dessert is strawberry shortcake, and this biscuit mix is a great start toward that summertime classic.

2 cups all-purpose flour
1 tablespoon baking powder
1/2 teaspoon salt
1/4 cup sugar

In a medium-size bowl, combine the ingredients. Store in an airtight container and label with a 3-month expiration date.

Berry Cobbler   *Serves 6 to 8*

4 cups fresh blueberries,
  raspberries, or boysenberries

1/4 cup fresh orange juice

1/4 cup sugar

1 teaspoon ground cinnamon

1 cup (2 sticks) unsalted butter,
  melted

1 large egg

One package Cobbler Mix

Preheat the oven to 375°F. In a large bowl, combine the berries, juice, sugar, and cinnamon. Place in a 13 x 9-inch baking dish. In a medium-size bowl, blend the butter and egg. Add the Cobbler Mix and stir until the mixture sticks together. Drop the cobbler topping by the tablespoon on the berries. Bake for 35 to 45 minutes, until the topping is golden brown and the filling is bubbling. Allow to cool for 15 minutes before serving.

Blueberry Popover Pancake   *Serves 6*

You can substitute fresh boysenberries or blackberries for the blueberries, if you like.

1/4 cup (1/2 stick) unsalted butter

1 cup milk

2 large eggs

1/4 cup sugar mixed with
  1/4 teaspoon ground cinnamon

1 package Blueberry Popover
  Pancake Mix

1 cup fresh blueberries

Warm maple syrup for serving

Preheat the oven to 450°F. Place 2 tablespoons of the butter in a 9-inch pie plate and place in the oven to melt the butter. Melt the remaining 2 tablespoons butter in the microwave or on the stovetop. Combine the melted butter, milk, eggs, and 2 tablespoons of the cinnamon sugar in a blender or food processor. Process for 30 seconds. Add the Blueberry Popover Pancake Mix and process until the mixture is smooth. Remove the pie plate from the oven, add the blueberries, and pour the batter over the berries. Sprinkle with the remaining cinnamon sugar. Bake for 20 minutes, reduce the oven temperature to 350°F, and bake for 10 to 15 minutes, until the pancake is golden brown. Cut into wedges and serve immediately with warm maple syrup.

Strawberry Shortcake   *Serves 12*

The biscuits are delicious with any type of berries and can even be spread with lemon curd and whipped cream when berries are not available.

1 package Strawberry Shortcake
  Mix

2 1/3 cups heavy cream

1 large egg, lightly beaten with 1
  tablespoon heavy cream

1/3 cup sugar

3 pints fresh strawberries, hulled
  and quartered

1. Preheat the oven to 425°F. Line a baking sheet with a silicone baking mat, parchment paper, or aluminum foil. Place the Strawberry Shortcake Mix in a large bowl and make a well in the center. Drizzle 1 1/3 cups of the cream over the mix and stir with a spatula or wooden spoon until the mixture begins to leave the sides of the bowl. Turn out onto a floured board and knead 5 or 6 times, until the dough comes together into a ball.

2. Flatten the dough into a circle approximately 8 inches in diameter and 3/4 inch thick. Cut the circle in half, then cut each half into 6 wedges. Place the wedges on the baking sheet, brush with the egg mixture, and sprinkle with a bit of the sugar. Bake for 14 to 16 minutes, until the tops and bottoms are golden brown. Remove from the oven and transfer to a wire rack to cool.

3. In a small bowl, beat the remaining 1 cup cream and 3 tablespoons of the sugar until the cream holds a soft shape. Sprinkle the remaining sugar over the berries. Split the shortcakes in half horizontally and spoon the berries over the bottom half of each. Top with some of the whipped cream and place the tops of the shortcakes on the whipped cream. Serve immediately.

Pizza Pizzazz Basket

Pizza is one of Americans' favorite fast foods, but once you've tasted a homemade pie, you'll never call the pizza delivery guy again. This terrific basket is a great gift for someone who has just moved into his or her first apartment, or it can be the perfect present for a wedding shower. To assemble the package, arrange the pizza dough mix on a pizza stone and add a package of Italian Herb Mix (page 103), a bottle of extra-virgin olive oil, a jar of sun-dried tomatoes, a wedge of Parmigiano-Reggiano cheese, a rotary cheese grater, and a pizza cutter. Wrap this all in a checked tablecloth or clear cellophane and decorate with red, white, and green ribbons. If funds are short, you can eliminate the pizza stone and arrange the pizza mix, herb mix, oil, and tomatoes in a basket, decorating it with colorful ribbons.

Pizza Dough Mix

Makes about 6 1/4 cups

2 packages active dry yeast
2 teaspoons sugar
6 cups all-purpose flour
2 teaspoons salt

In a large bowl, combine the ingredients. Store in an airtight container and label with a 3-month expiration date.

Pizza Margherita   *Makes two 14-inch pizzas*

2 cups warm water (105° to 115°F)
1/4 cup extra-virgin olive oil
3/4 cup freshly grated Parmesan cheese
1 package Pizza Dough Mix

1 1/2 cups pizza sauce, store-bought or homemade
2 cups shredded mozzarella cheese
1 tablespoon dried oregano

1. In a large bowl, combine the water, 2 tablespoons of the oil, 1/2 cup of the Parmesan, and the Pizza Dough Mix. Beat with a wooden spoon until the mixture forms a ball. Turn out onto a floured board. Knead until smooth and elastic, about 5 minutes. Place in an oiled bowl, cover with plastic wrap or a clean kitchen towel, and let rise until doubled in bulk, 45 minutes to 1 hour.

2. Preheat the oven to 425°F. Divide the dough in half and roll each half out on a floured board into a 14-inch circle. Lightly oil 2 pizza pans. Lay the dough in the pans and top with the sauce, mozzarella, and remaining 1/4 cup Parmesan. Crumble the oregano and sprinkle it over the top. Drizzle with the remaining 2 tablespoons olive oil. Bake for 15 to 20 minutes, until the cheese is golden and the crust is crisp. Serve immediately.

Spooky Halloween Basket

This delicious basket filled with treats is the perfect gift when visiting friends on Halloween, or use the goodies for any fall get-together. Pack a basket with small pumpkins for carving, fresh apples and caramels to make Caramel Apples, your homemade Peter's Pumpkin Bars, and Caramel Nut Popcorn Balls. Include your favorite book or CD of scary stories and face paints, if you like.

Peter's Pumpkin Bars

Makes 40 bars

Sweet and spicy with a creamy orange frosting, these bars are a winner all year long.

4 large eggs
1²/₃ cups sugar
1 cup canola oil
2 cups cooked pumpkin, or one 16-ounce can pumpkin puree
2 cups all-purpose flour
2 teaspoons baking powder
2 teaspoons Pumpkin Pie Spice Mix (page 131)
1 teaspoon baking soda
1 recipe Orange Cream Cheese Frosting

Preheat the oven to 350°F. Coat a 15 x 10-inch jellyroll pan with nonstick cooking spray. In a large bowl using an electric mixer, beat together the eggs, sugar, and oil. Gradually add the pumpkin, beating until smooth. Add the flour, baking powder, Pumpkin Pie Spice Mix, and baking soda and stir until smooth. Pour the batter into the prepared pan and bake for 20 to 25 minutes, until a cake tester inserted in the center comes out clean. Let cool completely, then frost and cut into bars. The bars will keep in an airtight container for up to 4 days.

Orange Cream Cheese Frosting

Makes about 3 cups

One 3-ounce package cream cheese, at room temperature
1/2 cup (1 stick) unsalted butter, softened
2 teaspoons orange extract
2 teaspoons grated orange zest
2¹/₂ cups confectioners' sugar

In a large bowl using an electric mixer, beat the cream cheese and butter until smooth. Add the extract, zest, and confectioners' sugar and continue to beat until the mixture reaches spreading consistency.

Caramel Nut Popcorn Balls

Makes 24 popcorn balls

Wrap these balls in orange and black cellophane and tie closed with coordinating ribbon for a Halloween treat.

2 quarts popped popcorn
One 6¹/₂-ounce can mixed nuts or nuts of your choice
4 cups firmly packed light brown sugar
1 cup light corn syrup
1/2 cup (1 stick) unsalted butter
1/2 cup water

Combine the popcorn and nuts in an 8-quart stockpot. In a large, heavy-bottomed pan, combine the remaining ingredients. Bring to a boil and cook over medium high heat until the mixture reaches 290°F on a candy thermometer. Pour the mixture over the popcorn and nuts and stir carefully until thoroughly coated. Roll the mixture into 2-inch balls and set on waxed paper or aluminum foil to cool. Wrap each individually in cellophane or plastic. The popcorn balls are best eaten within 2 days.

Caramel Apples   *Makes 5 apples*

5 medium-size apples
Wooden sticks

48 caramel candies
2 tablespoons water

Wash and dry the apples and remove the stems. Insert a stick into the stem end of each apple. Unwrap the caramels and place in a 2-quart saucepan over low heat. Add the water and stir until the caramels are melted and smooth, about 5 minutes. Dip each apple into the hot caramel sauce, twirling until coated. Scrape any excess sauce from the bottom of the apple into the pan. Place the dipped apples on waxed paper or aluminum foil sprayed with nonstick cooking spray to cool. The apples will keep, covered, in the refrigerator for up to 2 days. Let stand at room temperature for 15 minutes before serving.

Gingerbread House Basket

This is a wonderful family gift to give at the holidays. A basket will hold a cast-iron gingerbread house plaque (available through Williams-Sonoma or Sur La Table; see Source Guide), a package of Gingerbread House Mix, a two-pound package of confectioners' sugar for the frosting, and assorted candies for decorating the completed house. Make sure to include a cardboard square to build the house on, as well as the instructions for baking and assembling the house. If younger children are involved, you may want to assemble graham cracker houses using Gingerbread House Frosting as glue. Place the dry houses in a basket along with confectioners' sugar to make more frosting and candies to decorate the houses.

Gingerbread House Mix
Makes enough for 1 gingerbread house

2/3 cup firmly packed light brown sugar
6 cups all-purpose flour
2 teaspoons baking soda
1/2 teaspoon ground cloves
1/2 teaspoon ground cinnamon
1/2 teaspoon ground ginger
1/2 teaspoon ground nutmeg
1 teaspoon salt

In a medium-size bowl, combine the ingredients. Store in an airtight container and label with a 3-month expiration date.

Gingerbread House

Makes 1 gingerbread house

1 package Gingerbread House Mix	1 cup dark molasses
1/2 cup (1 stick) unsalted butter, softened	1/4 cup milk

1. Preheat the oven to 350°F. Coat one side of a gingerbread plaque with nonstick cooking spray. Place the Gingerbread House Mix in a large bowl. Make a well in the center and add the butter, molasses, and milk. Stir with a wooden spoon until the mixture begins to leave the sides of the bowl. Turn out onto a floured board and knead. It should be stiff.

2. Press half the dough into the prepared plaque. Bake for about 20 minutes, until browned. Remove the pieces from the plaque and cool on a rack. Allow the plaque to cool before baking the rest of the dough.

3. Spray the other side of the plaque with nonstick cooking spray. Press the remaining dough into the prepared plaque. Bake as above. Allow the gingerbread to cool completely before assembling the house.

Gingerbread House Frosting

Makes about 4 1/4 cups, enough for 1 gingerbread house

This royal icing is the glue that holds the house together and allows you to attach decorations.

2 large egg whites	4 cups confectioners' sugar

In a large bowl using an electric mixer, beat the egg whites and confectioners' sugar until stiff. Cover with a damp paper towel until ready to use.

Assembling the Gingerbread House

Assembling the walls the night before helps to stabilize the house. A cardboard cake board makes a solid base. It's better to decorate the roof before attaching it to the decorated house. Remember that every time you add frosting to the house, it adds moisture and makes the house less stable. Try to let the frosting dry before adding more.

This is a wonderful time to put a child's imagination to work. The frosting allows much freedom for error; cracks can always be camouflaged with more "snow." To make a pastry bag, put the frosting in a plastic bag and cut off one corner. Embellishments can be traditional candies, round striped mints, Necco wafers for roofing tiles, licorice, M&M's, gummy bears, jellybeans, or any of your favorite candies. Shredded wheat cereal makes a darling thatched roof, and pretzel sticks and Chex cereals are other great additions.

To assemble the house, use frosting to attach the bottom of each wall section to the cardboard base. Once all the walls are attached, fill in the spaces between them with frosting to secure them in place. Allow the frosting to dry completely. Decorate the walls and allow to dry completely. While the walls are drying, decorate the roof sections and allow to dry completely. Attach the roof sections to the walls with frosting and allow to dry completely. Decorate the cardboard base with frosting "snow" and candy "trees." The finished house will keep for about 1 month.

Thanksgiving Basket

If you are invited to Thanksgiving dinner, this is the gift to bring. Tuck packages of Dried Cranberry Sauce Mix and Pumpkin Pie Spice Mix into a pumpkin-shaped soup tureen or a basket lined with a colorful dishtowel. Include some whole nuts, citrus fruits, and apples in the basket, and add some seasonal cocktail napkins and taper candles in fall colors.

Dried Cranberry Sauce Mix

Makes about 2 1/4 cups

These dry ingredients make a deliciously piquant sauce to serve with poultry or pork.

1 cup firmly packed light brown sugar
1 tablespoon cornstarch
1 teaspoon chicken bouillon granules, or 1 chicken bouillon cube, crumbled
1 cup unsweetened dried cranberries
1 teaspoon dried thyme

In a medium-size bowl, combine the ingredients. Store in an airtight container and label with a 3-month expiration date.

Pumpkin Pie Spice Mix

Makes about 1/2 cup

A sprinkle of this mix adds just the right amount of spice to pumpkin, pear, or apple desserts.

1/4 cup ground cinnamon
2 tablespoons ground ginger
1 tablespoon ground cloves
1 tablespoon ground nutmeg

In a small bowl, combine the ingredients. Store in an airtight container and label with a 6-month expiration date.

Cranberry Sauce Makes about 2 3/4 cups

1/2 cup white wine
One 4-ounce can mandarin orange segments, drained, with juice reserved
1/2 cup fresh orange juice

1 package Dried Cranberry Sauce Mix
1 tablespoon chopped fresh parsley

In a 2-quart saucepan, heat the wine, the reserved juice from the mandarin oranges, and the orange juice over medium heat. Add the Dried Cranberry Sauce Mix and mandarin oranges and simmer, stirring occasionally, for 25 to 30 minutes, until the cranberries are softened and the sauce is thickened. Stir in the parsley and let cool to room temperature. Serve immediately or refrigerate for up to 2 weeks.

Pumpkin Pie *Makes one 9-inch pie*

2 large eggs

2 cups cooked pumpkin or one
  16-ounce can pumpkin puree

3/4 cup sugar

1 1/2 teaspoons Pumpkin Pie Spice
  Mix

1 2/3 cups light cream, half-and-half,
  or evaporated milk

One 9-inch pie shell

Whipped cream for garnish

Preheat the oven to 425°F. In a large bowl, whisk the eggs, pumpkin, sugar, Pumpkin Pie Spice Mix, and light cream together until blended. Pour the custard into the pie shell and bake for 15 minutes. Reduce the heat to 350°F and bake for about 45 minutes, until a knife inserted in the center comes out clean. Let cool and serve at room temperature, garnished with whipped cream. This pie will keep, covered, in the refrigerator for up to 3 days.

Applesauce Cake *Makes 1 loaf cake*

This cake, which improves with age, is a stellar addition to your recipe file.

1/2 cup (1 stick) unsalted butter,
  softened

1 cup granulated sugar

1/2 cup firmly packed light brown
  sugar

1 cup applesauce

1/2 cup lowfat plain yogurt

2 cups all-purpose flour

1 1/2 teaspoons Pumpkin Pie Spice
  Mix

2 teaspoons baking soda

Preheat the oven to 350°F. Coat an 8-inch loaf pan with nonstick cooking spray. In a large bowl using an electric mixer, cream together the butter and sugars. Add the applesauce and yogurt and blend until smooth. Add the flour, Pumpkin Pie Spice Mix, and baking soda, stirring to blend. Pour the batter into the prepared pan and bake for 50 to 60 minutes, until a toothpick inserted in the center comes out clean. Let cool on a wire rack for 1 hour before removing from the pan. Refrigerate until ready to slice. This cake will keep in the refrigerator for 5 days.

Happy Hanukkah Basket

Hanukkah is one of the most joyous festivals in the Jewish calendar, a time when music, games, and delicious food combine for an eight-day celebration. Traditional foods include potato pancakes, assorted vegetables, and beef brisket. Beef Brisket Marinade Mix is an appropriate contribution to the feast. Place it in a white basket lined with royal blue napkins and include a bottle of kosher wine, candles for the menorah, and a dreidel and chocolate coins wrapped in gold foil for the kids.

Beef Brisket Marinade Mix

Makes about 1/4 cup

8 juniper berries, crushed
2 bay leaves
1 1/2 teaspoons dried basil
1 teaspoon dried rosemary
1 teaspoon dried thyme
1 teaspoon garlic powder
1 teaspoon salt
1/4 teaspoon freshly ground black pepper

In a small bowl, combine the ingredients. Store in an airtight container and label with a 3-month expiration date.

Holiday Beef Brisket   *Serves 8*

One 750-milliliter bottle dry white wine
1 cup port wine
1 cup chopped onion, plus 1 large onion, chopped
4 cloves garlic, chopped, plus 2 cloves garlic, chopped
1 package Beef Brisket Marinade Mix

One 5-pound flat-cut beef brisket
2 tablespoons olive oil
4 medium-size carrots, sliced
2 medium-size ribs celery, chopped
Salt and freshly ground black pepper

1. Combine the wines, 1 cup chopped onion, 4 cloves garlic, and Beef Brisket Marinade Mix in a large saucepan over high heat and bring to a boil. Remove from the heat and let cool. Place the brisket in a 13 x 9-inch glass baking dish or 2-gallon zipper-top plastic bag. Pour the cooled mixture over the brisket. Cover the dish or seal the bag and refrigerate overnight.

2. Preheat the oven to 300°F. Drain the brisket from the marinade and discard the marinade. Heat the oil in a roasting pan over high heat and add the brisket, browning it evenly on all sides. Add the remaining chopped onion, the carrots, celery, and remaining 2 cloves garlic. Sauté for about 3 minutes, until the vegetables begin to color. Cover the pan, transfer to the oven, and roast for 4 hours.

3. Remove the brisket from the pan and skim any fat from the pan juices. Slice the meat thinly across the grain. Strain the pan juices and taste for salt and pepper. Pour the pan juices over the brisket and serve.

Ring in the New Year Basket

A few libations to help ring in the new year make a unique gift for your holiday host. Include two bottles of red wine, with a package of Glühwein Mix attached to one bottle and a package of Glogg Mix attached to the other. Don't forget to add a package of Grandpa Jim's Eggnog Mix in a decorative bottle, along with a nutmeg grater or microplane and a bag of whole nutmegs. Pack it all into a wine caddy or insulated reusable tote, decorate with ribbons, and tie paper party hats and noisemakers to the ribbons to top off your package. Or pack a picnic hamper with your special wines (and mixes) and Grandpa Jim's Eggnog Mix. Include tempered glasses for the mulled wine, wine charms to keep the drinks straight, and cute cocktail napkins to complete your gift.

Grandpa Jim's Eggnog Mix

Makes about 1 quart

1¹/₂ cups bourbon
1¹/₂ cups dark rum
1¹/₂ cups brandy
2 teaspoons vanilla extract
2 whole nutmegs
Four 4-inch cinnamon sticks, broken in half
8 whole cloves

Pour the liquor into an attractive 1-quart bottle. Add the spices and cork the bottle. Allow to stand in a cool, dark place for 2 weeks. Label with a 4-month expiration date.

Glühwein Mix

Makes about 2¹/₄ cups

This mix will be a welcome treat during the holidays.

2 cups sugar
1¹/₂ teaspoons ground cinnamon
1 tablespoon whole allspice berries
1 teaspoon ground cloves
¹/₂ teaspoon ground nutmeg
1 teaspoon dried orange peel

In a small bowl, combine the ingredients. Store in an airtight container and label with a 4-month expiration date.

Glogg Mix

Makes about 1¹/₂ cups

This pungent, festive drink mix includes raisins and spices.

³/₄ cup dark raisins
1 tablespoon whole cardamom seeds
1 tablespoon whole cloves
Two 4-inch cinnamon sticks, broken in half
¹/₂ cup sugar

In a small bowl, combine the ingredients. Store in an airtight container and label with a 2-month expiration date.

Eggnog   *Serves 12*

8 large egg yolks
1/2 cup sugar
2 1/2 cups chilled whipping cream

1 cup Grandpa Jim's Eggnog Mix
Freshly grated nutmeg and
  whipped cream for garnish

In a large bowl using an electric mixer, beat the egg yolks and sugar until pale yellow. Add the whipping cream and continue to beat. Add Grandpa Jim's Eggnog Mix and blend. Serve immediately, garnished with nutmeg and whipped cream.

Glogg   *Serves 4 to 6*

Glogg is a Swedish drink that will warm you on a cold evening.

One 750-milliliter bottle dry red wine
1 1/2 cups water
1 package Glogg Mix

2 tablespoons dark raisins for
  garnish
1 tablespoon sliced almonds for
  garnish

In a medium-size saucepan, combine the wine, water, and Glogg Mix. Bring to a boil over high heat, then remove from the heat and strain out the spices. Serve in mugs, garnished with the raisins and almonds.

Glühwein   *Serves 4 to 6*

Glühwein is a Bavarian drink traditionally served as an après-ski warmer.

One 750-milliliter bottle dry red wine
1/2 cup Glühwein Mix
1 navel orange, halved and thinly
  sliced

1 lemon, halved and thinly sliced
Orange and lemon slices for
  garnish

In a 3-quart saucepan, heat the wine and Glühwein Mix over medium heat, stirring to dissolve the sugar. Add the sliced orange and lemon and heat through, about 10 minutes. Remove from the heat and strain out the spices and fruit. Serve in tempered glass mugs, garnished with fresh orange and lemon slices.

SOURCE GUIDE

Containers and Ingredients

Basketville
www.basketville.com
800-258-4553

Bed Bath & Beyond
www.bedbathandbeyond.com
800-GOBEYOND (462-3966)

The Container Store
www.thecontainerstore.com
888-CONTAIN (266-8246)

Cost Plus World Market
www.costplus.com
510-893-7300

Crate and Barrel
www.crateandbarrel.com
800-967-6696

Great News!
www.discountcooking.com
888-478-2433

Hallmark
www.hallmark.com

HomeGoods
www.homegoods.com
800-614-HOME (4663)

iTunes
www.apple.com/itunes

King Arthur Flour
www.kingarthurflour.com
800-827-6836

Levenger
www.levenger.com
800-667-8034

Linens 'n Things
www.lnt.com
866-568-7378

Michaels
www.michaels.com
800-MICHAELS (642-4235)

Off the Deep End
www.offthedeepend.com
800-248-0645

Penzeys Spices
www.penzeys.com
800-741-7787

Pier 1 Imports
www.pier1.com
800-245-4595

Pottery Barn
www.potterybarn.com
888-779-5176

Sur La Table
www.surlatable.com
800-243-0852 (orders)
866-328-5412 (customer service)

Wild About Baskets
www.wildaboutbaskets.com
877-874-5740

Williams-Sonoma
www.williams-sonoma.com
877-812-6235

Gourmet Foods

Cook Flavoring Company
(vanilla powder)
www.cooksvanilla.com
800-735-0545

Dean & Deluca
www.deandeluca.com
800-221-7714

Murray's Cheese Shop
www.murrayscheese.com
888-MY-CHEEZ (692-4339)

Saco Foods
(powdered buttermilk)
www.sacofoods.com
800-373-7226

World Beer Direct
www.worldbeerdirect.com
800-609-ALES (2537)

Cookbooks

Jessica's Biscuit
www.ecookbooks.com
800-878-4264

Gardening Supplies

Gardeners Eden
www.gardenerseden.com
866-430-3336 (orders)
800-822-1214 (customer service)

Smith & Hawken
www.smithhawken.com
800-940-1170

Stickers

Mrs. Grossman's
www.mrsgrossmans.com
800-429-4549

Information About Gift Baskets

Gift Basket Review magazine
www.festivities-pub.com
800-729-6338

National Specialty Gift Association
www.nsgaonline.com
813-671-4757

INDEX

Note: *Italicized* page numbers indicate photographs.